MW01130301

ACTIONBOOKS
Notre Dame, Indiana 2014

Action Books
356 O'Shaughnessy Hall
Notre Dame, IN 46556

actionbooks.org

Joyelle McSweeney and Johannes Göransson, Editors
Paul Cunningham and Nichole Riggs, 2014-2015 Editorial Assistants
Andrew Shuta, Book Design

Cover image: Harold Cohen/AARON, "060927."

First Edition

ISBN: 978-0-9898048-44

Library of Congress Control Number: 2014946905

Action Books is generously supported by the College of Arts and Letters at the University of Notre Dame.

WILD GRASS
ON THE RIVERBANK

Hiromi Itō

Translated by Jeffrey Angles

TABLE OF CONTENTS

NOTE ABOUT JAPANESE NAMES

Except on the cover and title page of this book, where the author's name appears in the Western order for ease of cataloguing, all names inside the book appear in the traditional Japanese order with the family name first, then the given name. In other words, in the traditional Japanese order, the author's name is Itō Hiromi.

TRANSLATOR'S PREFACE

Born in Tokyo in 1955, Itō Hiromi is one of the most important poets of contemporary Japan. Itō rose to prominence in the 1980s with a series of dramatic collections of poetry that described sexuality, pregnancy, and feminine erotic desire in powerful direct language. Her willingness to deal with touchy subjects such as post-partum depression, infanticide, and queer sexual desire shocked Japan—a nation that was until that time more used to images of women as proud wives, mothers, and quiet care-givers—and earned attention from detractors who decried her subject matter, as well as feminist critics who lauded her as a heroine.

Because Itō was so willing to write about these subjects, she quickly became the foremost voice of the so-called "women's boom" of poetry in the 1980s.[1] Fellow poet Kido Shuri describes Itō's position in contemporary Japanese letters this way:

> The appearance of Itō Hiromi, a figure that one might best call a "shamaness of poetry" (shi no miko), was an enormous event in post-postwar poetry. Her physiological sensitivity and writing style, which cannot be captured within any existing framework, became the igniting force behind the subsequent flourishing of "women's poetry" (josei shi), just as Hagiwara Sakutarō had revolutionized modern poetry with his morbid sensitivity and colloquial style.[2]

The comparison between Itō and Hagiwara Sakutarō (1886-1942), a figure sometimes called the "father of modern Japanese poetry," suggests the colossal importance of Itō's contribution to contemporary poetry.

In the late 1980s, Itō's relationship with her husband Nishi Masahiko, a scholar of European and postcolonial literature, was failing, and she decided to divorce him and come to America to start anew. One reason Itō chose America in particular was her growing passion for Native American poetry, which she had first encountered a few years earlier in Japanese translations by Kanaseki Hisao. Her interest in Native American poetry led her to the work of Jerome Rothenberg, the avant-garde poet who had published several key collections of Native American poetry and helped make "ethnopoetics" a major force in contemporary American poetic circles. In 1990 Itō met Rothenberg when he visited Japan, and in 1991 she traveled with her two daughters to the University of California at San Diego where he was teaching.

The sojourn in California was a turning point in Itō's life. She quickly settled into life in America, making friends and building a home, although her somewhat rudimentary English meant that she maintained a strong sense of being a resident alien in a foreign environment. She traveled back and forth between Japan and America repeatedly, each time staying in the States on a three-month-long tourist visa before returning to Japan again. In 1997, she finally gained permanent residency and settled in America with her current partner, the British artist Harold Cohen. Since then, Itō has lived in Encinitas, a quiet city near San Diego, with Cohen, the two daughters she brought from Japan, and one more daughter whom the couple had together.

The change of setting led to several significant changes in her writing in terms of both genre and theme. Her already prodigious output of essays increased, and she began writing novellas. When asked about this shift, she typically mentioned it was because she was tired of the strictures of poetry and because she felt prose was better suited to exploring her new experiences as an immigrant. A number of these novellas explore the experience of migrants who, after being transplanted into a new environment, search for a new identity and modes of self-expression even while caught between languages.[3] In many cases, Itō refracts these issues through a feminist lens, writing articulately about the status accorded female migrants, especially those whose lack of English has condemned them to silence.

KAWARA AREKUSA

The long, narrative poem *Kawara Arekusa* (*Wild Grass on the Riverbank*) is 140 pages in the original Japanese and represents Itō's dramatic return to poetry after several years of writing prose. After being serialized in the prominent Japanese poetry journal *Gendai shi techō* (*Handbook of Modern Poetry*) in 2004 and 2005, the work was published in book form in 2005. It immediately earned significant critical praise and won the coveted Takami Jun Prize, a literary award given each year in Japan to an outstanding and innovative book of poetry. Critic Tochigi Nobuaki has written that in *Kawara Arekusa*, "we, Itō's readers, are witnessing the advent of a new poetic language that modern Japanese has never seen."[4]

One of the reasons for Tochigi's high appraisal is that the book breaks down the traditional distinctions between poetry and prose, challenging readers with a new, organic, seemingly spontaneous style of writing that blurs the boundaries of genre. With its unusual combination of short lines, run-on sentences, repetition, childish language, and Anglicized turns-of-phrase, Itō challenges notions of what might be considered "poetic," forging a unique style that is completely her own. Meanwhile, her language draws upon a dazzling range of references, borrowing from sources as disparate as medieval Japanese legend, jump rope songs, and lyrics from American pop music.

In addition to its innovative diction, *Kawara Arekusa* also represents one of the first attempts to write a book-length narrative poem in modern Japan. Whereas English-language poetry has a rich tradition of long, narrative poems by canonical authors like John Milton, Henry Wadsworth Longfellow, Samuel Taylor Coleridge, William Carlos Williams, and James Merrill, very few modern Japanese poets have attempted narrative poetry on such a large scale. Instead, most modern and contemporary Japanese poetry consists of smaller-scale works that present individual thoughts, feelings, or ideas rather than plot-driven tales. The ambitious scale, vibrant plot, and linguistic playfulness of Itō's book make it unlike any other work written in the entirety of modern Japanese poetry.

Itō has been fascinated by narrative poetry since at least 1992, the year she published her collection *Kazoku āto (The Art of Family)*. There, one finds a series of prose poems, each several pages long, in which she describes the inner workings of her family and of families in general in the form of short narrative poems. This and other collections written about the same time show that Itō was drawing a great deal of inspiration from Native American oral poetic traditions and from the medieval religious Japanese storytelling art of *sekkyō-bushi*. As R. Keller Kimbrough describes in his book *Wondrous Brutal Fictions*, *sekkyō-bushi* were religious stories that wandering storytellers and priests told on bridges, crossroads, temples, shrines—

just about anyplace where people naturally gathered.⁵ These medieval performances incorporated elements of prose, poetry, and song, sometimes accompanied by basic rhythmic accompaniment. The stories themselves are extended, elaborate folktales that revolve around famous Buddhist icons and describe the magical workings of prayer, fervent religious belief, and karma. The protagonists of these stories are frequently children or adolescents, but despite their young age, they undergo appalling hardships, and in some cases are even sold into slavery. Often with the help of divine intervention, the brutalized children manage to transcend their difficulties, find peace and sometimes even punish their torturers. In order to capture the attention of their pre-modern audiences, storytellers embellished these tales with surprising plot twists, cruelty, grotesquerie, and melodramatic moments of reconciliation. In the seventeenth century, the most important of these stories were recorded and published in written texts, which have come down to us today.

Kawara Arekusa does not deal with religious themes, but it does borrow from sekkyō-bushi in many noteworthy ways. The strange, surreal, and sometimes horrifying elements that one frequently finds in sekkyō-bushi are in ample evidence in Itō's text. For example, in her story, the stepfather of the protagonist experiences a strange sickness, dies, and undergoes a monstrous metamorphosis that leaves him a maggot-filled corpse that still manages to wheeze and talk as if it is still alive. These scenes drew their inspiration from a sekkyō-bushi called Oguri Hangan about a man who devolves into a horrifying, half-formed creature that has no choice but to rely on others for help.

Itō's tale, like many sekkyō-bushi, features a young protagonist who is a preteen at the time the work begins. In typical sekkyō-bushi fashion, she and her siblings suffer terribly over the course of the work. Perhaps the most famous of the medieval sekkyō-bushi is the story Sanshō Dayū (Sanshō the Bailiff), in which an older sister and her younger brother undertake a tremendous journey, get separated from their parents, and are sold into slavery. In her long narrative poem, Itō makes explicit reference to this story, naming the narrator's little brother Zushiō after the younger brother in Sanshō Dayū. Although the parents in Itō's tale are not entirely absent, the mother is so self-involved that she becomes neglectful to the point of abuse, allowing her children to fend for themselves for months on end.

Eventually, the children do manage find their way to personal redemption, but it is not through a *deus ex machina* ending like one finds in many *sekkyō-bushi*. Instead, it is through the sheer strength, determination, and independence of the protagonist that the children make their way to a place where they can lead a better life. In other words, Itō has departed from the thematic structure of *sekkyō-bushi* to create a new, more feminist story appropriate for our modern age. Instead of relying on outside help, the protagonist manages to find salvation and rebirth on her own.

The narrator of Itō's work is never explicitly identified by name, although Itō has commented in casual conversations that the section of the book entitled "Kawara Natsukusa" has a hidden double meaning. On the most literal level, *kawara* means "riverbank" and *natsukusa* means "summer grass." When combined, they sound like the formal name of some grassy plant that Itō has invented for this section of the poem. On the other hand, Kawara Natsukusa could also be name for a person (albeit an unusual one) in which "Kawara" acts as a surname and "Natsukusa" as the given name. In fact, Itō has often uses the name "Natsukusa" in her essays and conversation as a shorthand way to identify the protagonist of this book.[6]

While much of the book reads like a myth or legend from another era, certain elements are clearly autobiographical in nature. At the beginning of the work, Natsukusa is traveling with her mother and little brother as her mother rushes around the world giving readings of her own poetry. When the mother reads her work in the opening passages, the quotes come from one of Itō's own poems, thus drawing an explicit parallel between the mother in the poem and Itō herself. In the book, the family eventually settles in a dry landscape identified in the poem as the "wasteland" (*arechi*)—a place that strongly resembles the dry landscape of southern California where Itō currently resides. In the book, however, tragedy ensues, and the family moves to a lush, overgrown place known as the "riverbank" (*kawara*), which resembles her second home in Kumamoto, the city in southern Japan where Itō still spends a significant portion of each year. In fact, right behind Itō's home in Kumamoto is a wild, overgrown riverbank that inspired the description of the riverbank in this work.

The decision to write not from her own perspective but from the vantage point of a child just growing into adulthood, however, leaves Itō plenty of room for fictionalization and invention. The language of the narrative is childlike and capricious—full of erratic rhythms, repetition, and staccato sentences, intermixed with longer, run-on bits of prose. For inspiration, Itō drew upon the hybrid, heavily Anglicized Japanese of her own daughters, who, like Natsukusa, grew up while traveling back and forth repeatedly between America and Japan. Numerous places in the original, especially the passages that contain speech, are written in Japanese that sounds like it was translated from English. The Japanese original contains unusually ordered sentences that approximate the word order of English and numerous pronouns, which often drop out of ordinary spoken Japanese. In addition, the narrative sometimes contains English words transliterated into Japanese script. For instance, the swearing of the stepfather in the wasteland is included in the text in hiragana script as *shitto* and *damu*, thus adopting the sounds of the unfamiliar but often repeated words into Japanese. For Japanese readers, the result is defamiliarizing—the text sounds as if it has been filtered through English before coming into Japanese.

Because the protagonist Natsukusa is separated by age, language, and gender from many of the structures of power that might give her the ability to control her own destiny, she is in almost every way alienated from her surroundings. As a result, the world seems to be an enormous and almost mythologically grand place to her. At the beginning of the work, she travels with her mother and younger brother to the strange and unfamiliar landscape of the "wasteland," where her mother starts a relationship with a man. Before long, her mother and stepfather have a baby girl, but the new husband dies and dries out, becoming desiccated like a mummy. For some time, the family continues to live with the decomposing corpse, but after it grows infested with maggots and other bugs, the family decides it is time for them to cross the ocean and return to the riverbank where they had once previously lived. There, they return to their original house, where they find the desiccated corpse of the children's original father.

Perhaps as a psychological reaction to the trauma of being uprooted and shuttled back and forth across the Pacific, Natsukusa and her siblings begin to see imaginary figures that are the personifications of the various wild plants growing on the riverbank. For instance, goldenrod *(Solidago altissima)*, fleabane *(Conyza sumatrensis)*, and other plants begin to move and interact with the children like people. When the children want to find out about these new "neighbors," they look at a plant guide and begin learning the long, difficult names for the plants, all of which are written in the katakana syllabary. To the children, the plant names sound like the names of people from another country, and they begin using the plant names as if they were foreigners living in their midst.

The most important of the personified plant characters is a girl named "Kawara Alexa," whose name literally means "riverbank" *(kawara)* "wild grass" *(arekusa)* and who gives the book its title. In this translation, the Japanese word *arekusa*, which Itō has invented for this character, has been spelled "Alexa" to give it the look of an English name. (In Japanese, *kusa* is pronounced in way that somewhat resembles the English sound *xa* as in "exact.") Indeed, Itō has commented that it was because this name has such an international ring that she chose it for the narrator's imaginary friend. The text never tells us specifically what kind of plant Kawara Alexa is, although there is one place toward the end of the work that uses the words *Kawara arekusa* to identify to the made-up genus-species to which Alexa belongs. (At Itō's request, this translation renders that word as *Alexa kawaransis*, a macaronic combination of Japanese and Latin.[7])

Before long, the children start spending all their time on the riverbank, and the plants serve as their constant companion. Eventually, the negligent mother is arrested for child abuse, and the authorities, who have found the desiccated corpse of the children's father, attempt to take the children into custody. Alexa releases their dogs on the authorities, while the children light fires in the grass and take weapons in hand to protect themselves.

Itō drew her inspiration for these scenes from the bizarre standoff with the McGuckin family that took place near Lake Pend Oreille, Idaho in 2001. In May of that year, JoAnn McGuckin delivered the emaciated, desiccated corpse of her dead husband Michael to a funeral home. The coroner listed the cause of death as malnutrition and dehydration as complications of untreated multiple sclerosis. When concerned authorities went to the McGuckin household, they found the mother and her six children living in utter poverty without running water and with minimal food. The mother was arrested for negligence, but attempts to take the children into custody for safekeeping provoked a standoff with the children who released dozens of angry dogs onto the police. The standoff lasted for several days until the children finally surrendered.

In Itō's narrative, however, the children do not surrender. Instead, when the police raid the family home, the children flee into the riverbank and hide. There in the overgrown wilderness of the riverbank, alone without their mother, they have no place to go. It is only once Natsukusa and her siblings have finally lost everything that she realizes what she has known all along—she cannot depend on her own mother, who is too wrapped up in her own life and her own needs to protect and care for them. It is at that point that Natsukusa finally makes the life-changing decision to take her life into her own hands and go back to the foreign wasteland where they used to live. Not coincidentally, it is at this moment of bold psychic resolve that Natsukusa's imaginary friend Alexa disappears. (Itō has commented that she derived her inspiration for Natsukusa's resolve from the female character Otohime in the medieval *sekkyō-bushi* text *Shintokumaru*).

Throughout the text, Itō uses the names of foreign plants that have been naturalized in both Japan and California. For instance, *Paspalum urvillei* (Vasey grass), *Verbena brasiliensis* (Brazilian verbena), *Conyza sumatrensis* (fleabane), and *Erigeron canadensis* (horseweed) are all native to the Americas, while *Sorghum halepense* (Johnson grass) comes from the Mediterranean and has been naturalized throughout the northern hemisphere. Itō has provided a short description of the stems, leaves, flowers, and habits of each of these plants at the back of the book. As she notes, all of these plants grow profusely on riverbanks, harbors, and abandoned strips of land and are often considered noxious weeds—undesirable, foreign, antisocial plants. Not coincidentally, all of these thrive in the two places where Itō lives.

Although frequently demonized as weeds, these plants serve as symbols of the vitality of displaced people who move and take root elsewhere—migrants who leave their point of origin, naturalize and learn to flourish within the harsh and frequently lonely environments of their new homes. Itō makes this metaphor especially explicit at the end of the work. When the plants take on personified forms and speak in the last chapter, they use the awkward speech of an immigrants speaking in a second language. In other words, Itō's long narrative poem can be read as a complex exploration of migration, adaptation, and emotional healing, all recounted in a surreal, eco-mythical mode of storytelling.

TRANSLATION STRATEGIES

Texts that use unusual language are always more difficult to translate than ones that use straightforward, simple language. While some translators might have chosen to render this translation into common, unobtrusive, and seemingly seamless English, doing so would have given a false view of what is happening in Itō's Japanese, which frequently uses defamiliarizing strategies to give the language a fresh, unusual flavor.

As mentioned above, the text frequently uses types of language that are not always considered "poetic," such as colloquialisms, contractions, slang, children's language, and run-on sentences. At the same time, however, the narrative sometimes includes difficult, formal expressions as well. The impression one gets is that Natsukusa is constantly learning from the adults around her and using expressions that she has picked up from their speech as she tries to survive in a negligent world that is too big for her. I have done my best to reproduce in this English translation the juxtapositions of speech belonging to different registers.

In the original Japanese, Itō keeps punctuation to a minimum, instead using line breaks to separate grammatical ideas. In the prose-like passages, she uses only commas to separate sentences, giving the impression that the words are flowing forth in an almost unbroken torrent. (In fact, when Itō reads from this work, she usually reads at a quicker than normal pace.) In addition, Itō uses few quotation marks. The result is the impression that all of the words, regardless of who utters them, are being filtered through the consciousness of the narrator, who is in turn conveying them to us, the readers. Rather than artificially adding punctuation or capital letters to separate sentences (Japanese has nothing that corresponds to capital letters), this translation replicates the loquaciousness of the original, unpunctuated Japanese.

As mentioned earlier, the characters frequently speak an Anglicized version of Japanese. Ordinarily, Japanese speakers drop the subject of the sentence and other pronouns, provided that those parts of speech are clear from context; however, Itō's characters frequently include them. In other places, Itō inverts ordinary word order, moving the verb from its ordinary position at the end of the Japanese sentence to an earlier spot close to the subject. The resulting language sounds like "translationese"—language born in the imagined space between the two languages. The inclusion of pronouns and scrambled word order are next to impossible to reproduce in English, which is much less forgiving about the use—or misuse—of pronouns and unusual word order than Japanese.

One of the greatest challenges came halfway through the text when the protagonist begins mentioning the names of the plants she has encountered by the river. In the Japanese original, the plant names are all written in the katakana syllabary, which is used for foreign names as well as plant names in modern Japan. A reader of the Japanese quickly realizes that the strange and unfamiliar plant names look like complicated foreign names to Natsukusa. After extensive consultation with Itō, I have decided to use the scientific Latin names for the plants in this translation. The reason is Latin names consists of two parts—the genus and the species—which could be construed as sounding like the first and last name of a person. This, we hoped, would contribute to the illusion that the plants are interacting with the children like people. Plus, Latin sounds quite formal and complicated to most English readers, just as the katakana names in the Japanese sound complex to most Japanese readers.

In Japanese, however, there are sometimes elements of plant names that are real, ordinary words, and that fact is not lost on Natsukusa. For instance, the word *hime-mukashi-yomogi*, meaning "horseweed" (*Erigeron canadensis*), is a combination of three words that mean "princess," "long ago," and "artemisia." About halfway through the book, Natsukusa begins playing with the plant names, breaking them apart into their component elements, and playfully rearranging them into phrases that at first glance seem like nonsensical nursery rhymes. Upon closer inspection, however, it becomes clear that Natsukusa's "nonsense" is a way of trying to come to grips with her own strange life in exile in the overgrown wasteland of the riverbank. She is quite literally trying to make sense out of the foreign names and phrases that have infiltrated her world, and in the process, she seeks her own place within it. In those passages, when the text gives an entire plant name, I include the scientific name in Latin, but when the plant names are broken into parts and used just as fragments, I have translated those component parts in a literal way wherever possible. For instance, when the text includes the complete plant name *hime-mukashi-yomogi*, I translate it as *Erigeron canadensis* (the scientific name for horseweed), but when the word hime appears alone, I translate it literally as "princess." Similarly, when the text says *ō-arechi-nogiku*, I translated it as *Conyza sumatrensis* (fleabane), but when the word *arechi* appears in isolation, I translate it as "wasteland." This is complicated by the fact that the narrator sometimes sprinkles in the word *no* among the various components. *No* is a Japanese particle that is used to connect nouns, as well as homophonic word that means "field," and so at first glance, it seems that Natsukusa is connecting her list of plant name components in inventive, new ways, as if to make sense out of them. At the same time, the word *no* sounds like what an English-speaker would use to correct him or herself. Similarly, the word *ō* which is sprinkled in from time to time, could either be the Japanese word meaning "big" or the English sound of recognition "oh." In other words, in those seemingly nonsensical, nursery-rhyme-like passages, the text is written in a way that could be read in two languages at once, although there is a gap between what the text would mean in each.

Although such passages might be seen as losing something in translation, it is my belief that something is also always gained when a text is translated, as words come together in new, unpredictable fashions to hint at possibilities that were only latent in the original, forging fresh alliances and bonds across the field of the text. It is my hope that this translation manages to replicate at least some of the idiosyncratic, linguistic playfulness of Itō's writing while at the same time allowing the text enough room to breathe and take on new life in English. In fact, in her 2014 book of essays *Kodama kusama (Echoes: Tree Spirits, Grass Spirits)*, Itō has commented that as she read my translation, she could not help feeling that the Japanese was a translation of the absent English original that had only been revealed by my act of translation. There, she states, "As I read out loud the English of the English translation, I feel as if that is really my true voice, and I am caught up in the illusion that this is the way that I have been telling the story since the very beginning. In other words, I cannot help but feel like the book *Kawara Arekusa* is merely a Japanese translation, and the original is the English."

Notes

[1] Readers can find translations of many of the poems from Itō's early career in Hiromi Itō, *Killing Kanoko: Selected Poems of Hiromi Itō*, translated by Jeffrey Angles (Notre Dame, IN: Action Books, 2009).

[2] Nomura Kiwao and Kido Shuri, *Sengo meishi sen II* (*Selection of famous postwar poetry II*), Gendai shi bunko tokushū han 2 (Tokyo:Shichōsha, 2001), 230.

[3] For a translation of one of Itō's novellas, see "House Plant," trans. Itō Hiromi and Harold Cohen, *U.S.-Japan Women's Journal*, special issue on Itō Hiromi, edited by Jeffrey Angles, no. 32 (2007): 115-63. This issue also contains additional articles and translations of Itō's work.

[4] Tochigi Nobuaki, "Wild Grass upon a Riverbank: Transformational Narratives by the Poet who goes into a Trance," *Poetry International Web*, 1 Oct 2006, http://japan.poetryinternationalweb. org/piw_cms/cms/ cms_module/index.php?obj_id=7853. For more of Tochigi's comments, see Tochigi Nobuaki, *Seishoku tsukai no shijin-tachi* (*Poets Whose Use the Color of Their Voices*) (Tokyo: Misuzu Shobō, 2010), 71-81.

[5] R. Keller Kimbrough, Introduction, in *Wondrous Brutal Fictions: Eight Buddhist Tales from the Early Japanese Puppet Theater* (Honolulu: University of Hawaii Press, 2013), 1-22. Kimbrough's book includes translations of three *sekkyō-bushi* that inspired different sections of Wild Grass on the Riverbank, namely *Sanshō Dayū, Oguri [Hangan],* and *Shintokumaru*.

[6] For instance, see Itō's comments about *Wild Grass in the Riverbank* in Itō Hiromi, *Kodama kusadama* (Tokyo: Iwanami Shoten, 2014), 133-40.

[7] See Itō Hiromi, *Kodama kusadama*, 140.

WILD GRASS
ON THE RIVERBANK

MOTHER LEADS US ON BOARD

Mother led us along
And we got on board
We got on, got off, then on again
We boarded cars and busses
Then we boarded planes
Then we boarded more busses and trains and cars

The place where we arrived was a building of muffled voices, it had a cold corridor where people had gathered in droves, they all looked confused, they all had a confused expression as if they had no idea what would happen next, they were sitting and staring with wide open eyes, the room became dark, and in the middle of it, mother's form rose up

Mother mumbled, her words a pitter-patter,
"I don't know what to do"
Mother tapped the floor with her wrinkled hand and whispered,
"We've been living like this since you were born"
She closed her eyes halfway, clutched at her breasts and railed,
"I've had nothing but hardship since I was born"
She repeated,
"I've had nothing but hardship since I was born"
My little brother began to sob
I asked him what's the matter
He said, I hate it here, I hate it here,
I don't want to see her
He said I want to run away and go home,
She's mean, she makes me sick, she's dirty,
She's a mess, she's dirty,
It's like she's rubbing off on us,
I don't want to see or hear her, I want to go home,
My little brother sobbed as he spoke

All the people had unfamiliar faces and sat in unfamiliar fashions, no one seemed to understand Japanese, mother was sitting alone on a stage, then she stood up and thumped her feet against the floor, to everyone else it was nothing but noise, then mother squeezed a noise from her mouth, to me it sounded more like a voice than a plain old noise, it had meaning, it had emotion, it was sad at moments and happy at others, it had meaning, it had meaning, but to all the other people, it was nothing but noise

Mother said,
"A growing, laughing, living body"
Mother repeated,
"A growing, laughing, living body"

Once I asked mother, do all those people understand?
Mother responded,
I don't think so
Why are you doing that if they don't understand?
Doesn't your voice just come out and go away?
Mother responded,
I wonder
Why do all those people come if they don't understand?
Mother responded,
They come because they don't understand, get it?
Mother repeated over and over,
"A living body, a living body"
Why do we come places where no one understands us?
Mother responded,
Maybe we can get some money
Mother repeated over and over,
"A living body, a living body"
Little brother said, I hate it here
I whispered, go to sleep
He put his head between his hands, covered his ears, closed his eyes
And before long he stopped moving
I was also starting to doze, little brother's eyes were closed
Still covering his ears, he fell sound asleep, and started to melt away

I was also starting to doze
"That is what I am, that is who I am"
The words repeated,
"That is what I am, that is who I am"
The voice stopped, mother gave a small laugh, and relieved, the listeners
laughed too

We were shaken awake, the men spoke to us in a language we didn't know,
my little brother and I didn't know how to respond, mother was speaking
to some people without turning to look at us, she spoke to more people
without turning to look at us, then hours later, mother finally looked back
and told us we're going, she led us to a hotel, without even combing our hair,
we crawled underneath the stiff sheets on the narrow bed and fell asleep,
my little brother was soft and warm, mother was hard and cold, mother and
I fell asleep holding him, we fell asleep, everyone touching everyone else's
arms and legs, during the night a dry, withered hand caressed me, I was so
tired I couldn't even brush the hand away when it pulled my ponytail

Mother led us along
And we got on board
We got in cars and busses and planes
Then we got on more busses and trains and cars
Little brother said, that was fun,
At one of the airports, we were waiting when the room we were waiting in
Turned into a bus and started moving then merged with the plane
But I didn't remember getting on anything like that

We slept here and there in the airports, we played here and there in the
airports, we tumbled over and bumped into things here and there in the
airports, I got scolded, my little brother cried, mother bought us food, we
didn't eat it all and threw it away, we coaxed mother for things and got
scolded, there were lots of families like us, parents gave their kids food to
eat, the kids got scolded by their parents, some of the families traveling
from airport to airport had their hair cut, some had it braided, some had
it tied up, some had it shaved right off, everyone was wearing different
colored clothes, everyone was waiting, everyone was spread out all over

the airport, waiting all over the place, every last one of them was waiting, the kids who were not eating or sleeping or waiting instead tumbled over, bumped into things, and played just like us

It was dark inside the planes
I watched the movies but the screen was either too close or too far away
In the next seat, little brother was slumped over asleep
Mother had covered him in the darkness
I watched the movies
People got angry and got killed
In a language I didn't understand
In the next seat, little brother was slumped over asleep
I thought she had fallen asleep, but mother started moving under the covers in the darkness with a certain monotonous rhythm, then she let out a long breath and stopped moving, when she did that I smelled the same sweet and sour scent as always, it was not the smell of passing gas, nor the smell of breast milk, nor the smell of my navel, after she let out a long breath and stopped moving, she fell asleep, I tried doing the same thing, I stretched out and spread out slowly, allowing me to sleep a little, allowing me to sleep just a little

I watched the movies
If I don't put on the earphones
I could get away without listening
To their angry shouts and death cries
In the next seat, little brother was slumped over asleep
In the darkness, mother wept silently to herself
Quietly, she wept to herself

When we got off the plane my little brother threw up
The long, long moving sidewalk clattered along
Mother held my brother who was covered in vomit and walked
She walked along the moving sidewalk with great speed
As the long, long conveyor belt clattered along

It took one day and one night to reach immigration, the route was lined with many, many immigrants who had run out of energy, collapsed along the way and shriveled up, no matter how wealthy the country, they never make the path to immigration any shorter, their wealth won't help us, there is just sadness, curt answers and pain, those places are nowhere in particular, and to make matters worse, there is no guarantee we'll even make it through, little brother didn't notice but I did, our passports were bad passports, I had noticed alright, at immigration in every country, the men made unfriendly faces and stared at their computers, that's because our passports are bad passports, little brother tried looking at the computer and got scolded, not just once, not just twice, the men pointed us to another window and told us to go there, we followed mother as she rushed us onward, not just once, not just twice, she dragged us to all sorts of places

As mother dragged us along
All sorts of things got pulled out
Telephone lines and books of telephone numbers and postcards
And old passports punched full of holes
And leftover airplane food and changes of pants and apples with missing bites and the tip of a dried-up hand
And small bottles full of bugs we'd collected
The bugs were dead inside the bottle
People called out to us
You dropped something, you dropped something
You dropped something, you dropped something, pick it up, pick it up
So we picked it up
And put it back where it belonged
Mother dragged us along
And when we got there, no one was there
So we waited before the empty window
There was no guarantee the window would open
Little brother asked, what'll we do if no one comes?
My mother responded, then this is where we'll live, and with that she smiled

In one corner of a great immigration hall, little brother was slumped over asleep in a row of hard chairs before an empty window, watching him was enough to put me to sleep too, something was pulling at me so I tried to brush it aside, it was that dried-up hand, the tip seemed to break when I brushed it aside, it made a dry sound as it fell to the ground, no sooner do I realize what's happened then someone shakes me awake, mother was standing up and saying we're ready to go, I asked if the bad part of our passport had gotten fixed, she told me no, she told me a bad passport is always bad, we went outside the airport, and as we put our three bad passports away, mother nudged and said, look we're going

Once again we were getting on board

But no matter how many times we arrived, our journey still did not end

MOTHER TAKES US TO THE WASTELAND WHERE WE SETTLE DOWN

Mother led us along and we got on board
We got on and off again
We boarded cars and busses and planes
Then we boarded more busses and trains and cars

I was beginning to think that life would go on like that forever, it would go on and on and on, but one day it stopped all of the sudden, that day wasn't especially different from all the others we spent on the busses, trains, cars and airplanes, we left the airport just like always, but this time mother smiled and ran up to someone, it was a man, he pressed his darkly tanned face covered with bushy whiskers against her face, he wriggled his tongue into her mouth, then he grabbed mother's breasts, shoulders, stomach, and hips and gave them a hard squeeze
Mother made little sucking sounds at the man's mouth
He closed his eyes and groaned as he tasted her saliva, inhaled her aroma, and stroked her skin and her flesh, then when he removed his mouth, he spread his arms wide and said *ohh mai ohh mai* and hugged me and my little brother and put us in a gigantic car, the sky was blue there, it was really, really blue, we drove for hours and hours beneath the blue sky before we arrived at the big house in the wasteland, there was a sprinkler in the yard, and it turned on at night
Ohh mai, it soaked everything in sight

Mother said, you all will sleep here, then went into the man's bedroom
At the crack of dawn, there was a loud noise, it was like the sound of a washrag sloshing around in a bucket of water, the slippery sliding sound of scrubbing, the sound of mother's voice as if she were singing or breaking down in tears, that happened over and over for days on end, at first it woke me up, but eventually I got used to it, and it didn't wake me up anymore
During the day, mother used a language we didn't understand to tell the man every teeny weeny thing my little brother and I said, then they started talking to us in that same language, at first I had no idea what they were talking about, but then eventually I got used to that too

Then mother started standing in unfamiliar stances, walking an unfamiliar walk, cooking unfamiliar foods that she made us eat, even though it was unfamiliar, it was good just because she was the one who made it, we realized we were gobbling it up left and right

Mother stank with an unfamiliar scent, that man was always at the dinner table, mother embraced and stroked us in unfamiliar ways, such things had certainly happened before, mother had settled down with a man and dragged us into it, and every time that happened, we were dragged right into the middle of it as if the whole thing were no big deal at all

Mother didn't get on board or go anywhere anymore, we didn't trail after mother any more, walking from airport to airport like our lives depended on it, one day the man used an unfamiliar name to call out to mother, she responded as if nothing was the matter at all, when we questioned her about it, mother said, you're just trying to find fault with his words

Who cares about a name as long as you've got one?

Words fulfill their usefulness as long as they get through

You two, mother said to us,

Let's not use Japanese any more

I was eleven, my little brother was eight
We stopped speaking
But when we spoke to each other or to mother
We used nothing but Japanese
We stopped speaking anything but Japanese
When people approached, we fell silent
And when they left, we started speaking again
We spoke Japanese
Japanese was all we had
We spoke only Japanese
I started pricking up my ears
Little brother did too
For years and years, we pricked up our ears
One day I asked my brother,
Can you hear something?
He answered,

I can't hear anything
I tried asking again,
Are you listening to something?
He answered,
I'm not listening to anything
For years on end, we pricked up our ears

One day when I woke up, there was a tiny car seat for a baby next to my
pillow, and in it is a fresh little baby, *ohh mai gossh*, a fresh little baby, I
asked, when did you get that? mother answered, yesterday, mother's belly
was still swollen like she still had more babies inside, babies she hadn't
given birth to yet, the baby started crying like a little cat, mother bared her
breast, it was an altogether unfamiliar shape, it had risen up and become
dark and fierce, it smelled so raw and fresh that I had to hold my breath,
the little baby shifted its little head and started sucking on it, mother took
out the other breast and exposed its heavy, swollen shape, right before our
eyes it began to bend and twist and the tip split open, and the milk flew
out making an arc, my brother screamed *eeewww*, mother said, try it, try
sucking it, it's sweet, you'll be sure to like it, we hesitated, but then mother
grabbed my little brother and forced it into his mouth, the breast looked
much bigger and fiercer than my little brother's head, and mother looked
even bigger and fiercer than that, the bubbling milk came squirting from its
smiling, split tip, with resignation he took it in his mouth, mother squeezed
and stroked it two or three times, I heard him swallowing one gulp after
another, *gurooosu*, he said, his mouth dripping with white milk

The wind changed directions
And blew in from the desert
Dry as a bone
A mountain burned in the distance
A mountain burned, raining down ashes
The ashes blocked out the sun
We could look at the sun with our naked eyes
The plants turned to corpses
Dry as a bone

The sage released its intense aroma
The rabbits and coyotes turned to corpses
Dry as a bone
When winter came bringing rain
Everything got wet, moss grew, things sprouted, flowers bloomed
The cacti and yucca grew long and lanky
Everything under the sky became a sea
Everyday the sun fell in the sea
Mother said, I'd like to start rowing, rowing over there to the other side of
the sea, she said this in Japanese, if we go over there, no one will ever tell
us to come back, mother stared at the sea

When we came here
I was eleven, my little brother was eight
Since then, we've used Japanese, or at least we tried to
But the sounds that drip out of our mouths
When just the two of us talk
Only emphasize how much we've forgotten
He and I push sounds out our mouths, we push out sounds with our lips
and palates
We extract them from our noses, catch them on our tongues
We let them spill out unintentionally
One day, little brother said,
I *katto* it, my finger,
It is, blood running, me alone
His words were a mixture of two languages
One day, my brother said,
Sis', what's my name? do you know?
I said to him,
It's Zushio
My brother said,
No one can pronounce it, not my name, absolutely not
No one can say my name at all
I repeated to him,
It's Zushio

The baby grew bigger and began blabbering in baby talk
Saliva dripping from its mouth the whole time
And it began forming words, as if to deride my brother's distress

This all happened long ago
When mother led my brother and I along
And we got on board
We got on and off and on again
We boarded cars and busses then planes
Then we boarded more busses and trains and cars
We got on board
And began to move
Still, no matter how often we got on board, our journey still did not end

WE LIVE IN THE WASTELAND

The winds of Santa Ana blew
The winds that blew from the desert
Were strong, hot, and dried up everything
They burned the mountains, burned the forests, and clouded the skies with
ash
And who was she? Who was Santa Ana?
Where did she come from?
Why did she burn everything
With such savage ferocity?
Was there something she hated?
Was she someone's mother?

The potted plants mother bought were all tropical vines, their leaves were
thick, and they grew with water and light, the ends of the vines grew long,
eventually the vines began to climb up on their own, if you supported
them on a pole, they'd climb up and up without stopping, if you didn't
support them, the vines would crawl all over the house, white mealy bugs
would cake themselves on all the big shoots like powder, mother watered
the vines and peeled off the bugs, she peeled them off with such, such
careful attention, and then that big, whiskery father got sick and started
laying in bed, he said that when Santa Ana's winds blew and dried out the
air, he felt like his whole body was coming apart, then when Santa Ana
stopped and the humidity returned, he said the joints of his dismembered
body all began to creak and grow sore, he had been tan and strong, but he
grew thin as a rail, and he hurt so much that he groaned in a pathetic voice,
and before long, he could no longer stand up by himself

The house stunk when you went inside
Chicken and moldy yogurt forgotten in the refrigerator
Little brother's shorts, baby sister's diapers, stale urine
Or the pile of shit little brother had left in the corner
When he couldn't hold it all night
The house stunk inside

And the vines crawled from window frame to window frame
Just outside, the sky was blue, the sea sparkled, the wind blew across the
wasteland
In the wasteland
The sage dried
Where it stood
The sage dried
Where it stood
We forgot what was happening inside and walked around
Little brother scratched his skin raw
The sage dried
Where it stood
No matter how bright it was outside
The house stunk when you went inside
It was shady and cold and the wind didn't blow through
The vines writhed their way across the house
Mother squatted and watered them
The vines sucked up the water, grew bold, and slid their way inside her
vagina
Mother walked around with the vines dangling from her vagina
Father let out a groan
Little brother scratched at his skin

Father called out mother's name
Come… here… please…
Father was wracked with coughing, *hack-hack, hack-hack*
Shitto, damu, he berated himself in a dry, raspy voice
Shitto, damu, shitto, damu
Father called mother
Come… here… please…
Mother stood up quickly and went into the bedroom
As if she wanted to have more and more babies, mother went into the
bedroom, even though if she were to get pregnant now, all of the babies
she'd give birth to would shrivel up and dry out, even though my newborn
baby sister was already covered in dry, little wrinkles

She kept going into the bedroom
But before she got pregnant again
The winds of Santa Ana started blowing again
Drying up everything
Man-eating bugs appeared in the house
Little brother scratched himself raw and began to bleed

One day, father died, he grew still, grew cold, his face grew bluish black, he began smelling like shit, in the kitchen mother spread a chicken's legs and pulled out a string of guts, there was a big hole in the chicken, mother stuffed it with lemons, one lemon, two lemons, three lemons, four lemons, any number of lemons could fit in there, mother roasted the chicken for an hour and a half, when she cut the chicken open, the lemons that had cooked down came spilling out, it took us twenty minutes to finish eating the chicken
I think he is dead, I said as I put away the dishes
I know, mother answered as she washed the pans
That evening the winds of Santa Ana began to blow again
Fanning everything with hot wind, drying out everything

We heard father's voice
A low voice, *ooooh, ooooh*
My little brother clung to me and cried out to me,
Is he dead? Maybe he's not?
When I went to ask
Mother went into the bedroom, caressed father, groaned, and gasped
She came out smiling
And said,
He's dead
Mother said,
There are spots appearing on his skin and voices coming out of his throat,
But there's no mistake, he's a corpse
Little brother scratched at his skin

Father's corpse stayed there on the bed like that, we all went about our

lives as usual, mother slept with father's corpse at night like usual, we did the same things as usual, and the days went by as the stench filled the house
The stench filled the whole house
I asked mother,
Why not bury or cremate father? Why not give him a funeral?
I asked mother,
Isn't that what you do, give a funeral when someone dies?
Mother said to me, next year, maybe he'll come back again

Eventually, mother moved to my bed, she said, this is because he stinks, mother slept with me, my bed was so small we had no choice but to hold one another while we slept, arms around each other, a very small bed, mother's very stinky neck, mother's stinky pillow
And father's corpse, which stunk even more
Mother said, I'll put him somewhere else until he stops stinking, so she dragged father's corpse, sheets and all, to the basement then closed the door, he left a trail behind him to the basement door like a slug
Little brother asked, did something happen to him?
Little sister asked, did something happen?
I hit my sister
She shrieked at me,
She hit me, she's mean to me

Santa Ana blew, the hot air made the bugs multiply in our house, little brother's whole body was eaten up, the stench was terrible, we went about our lives with every window open, every possible thing we could open was wide open, but still the flies buzzed around us, we lived just like always, the stench was terrible, we ate our meals over and over, we went to sleep over and over, my brother scratched himself to bits, the flies buzzed around us, when we went to sleep we shut all the entrances into the bedroom, all we had was the corpse, I smashed the flies with a damp rag, I made a pile of flies, the stench was terrible

Little brother asked, what happened to him?
Little sister asked, what happened?

Mother asked, you want to open the door? he doesn't stink at all, (...no) not any more
So mother opened the door at the top of the stairs
The stench pierced our nostrils
We couldn't get the door in the basement open
Something was stuck
Mother shook the door, it came off, and we fell into the basement
And there was the corpse
Father, in other words
Father as a corpse
I jumped back
Little brother let up a wail, a high-pitched, long cry
The corpse was dried up, the hair had fallen out, the stomach had swollen up, the eyes had sunken in
Something was wriggling in the back of his eye sockets
Mother said, he isn't dead
Mother gently brought her cheeks and lips close, as if he was made of bubbles or something fragile she didn't want to break
Mother stuck her tongue into the corpse's lips
Father's corpse made a sound and sucked on it

Mother took care of the corpse while taking care of the vines, like the vines that grew tangled up in one another, father's corpse got tangled with mother, mother got tangled in father's corpse, mother grew new shoots and the vines proliferated, she used a cotton swab to scrape up the white mealy bugs and kill them, father eventually got used to the fact that he was a corpse, he regained his fatherliness, the first step was making a sound from his dead throat, he did it for the whole family
Damu itto, damu itto
As the corpse's face contracted, a huge number of wrinkles appeared on it, a sound came out as the wrinkles expanded and contracted, it would have been a voice if he had been doing it voluntarily
Damu itto, damu itto
Father was angry, he was angry at a world that didn't behave like he wanted, at our family that didn't behave like he wanted, I remembered

that fathers are supposed to be angry, it doesn't matter who he is, all fathers are always angry at their children, it's just a part of life like eating a meal or taking a shit, and we, the ones who bear the brunt of our father's anger, realize how completely powerless we are, we are helpless, we are overcome by loneliness, and we break down in tears, how did we end up like this with him watching over our family like this? I tried to remember, but in my memories, the people I had called father were always like that, always stinky, always a corpse, dried up and ugly, unable to do anything but still they would keep watch over us and yell at us loudly, I think to myself,

> *Let's go home, leave father and go*
> *Let's go across the ocean*
> *If we do, no one will tell us to come back ever again*

Our corpse father cries out, *damu itto, damu itto*
And mother rushes right to him
What's the matter? What's the matter?
Damu itto (My wife has no sense of judgment, the kids are dumb and reckless)
Damu itto (I'm the only one who's right)
What's the matter? What's the matter?
Damu itto (I'm right)
Damu itto (I'm the only one who's right)
What's the matter? What's the matter?
With vines still hanging from her vagina
With several vines still hanging there
Mother draws close to father and touches him

ABANDONMENT

Mother was always ferocious
And full of hatred for someone
Mother was always hungry and wanted to eat
Didn't matter what
Didn't matter whom
That was mother

The winds of Santa Ana blew
Our faces and eyes and lips grew bone dry and tightly stretched
Mother's hair grew gray
Small wrinkles appeared on her hands and face
And then the white mealy bugs began to multiply even more quickly
The new shoots, the bases of the leaves, the backs of the leaves, the space
between the veins on the leaves, and even the vines themselves got so
caked with bugs that they turned completely white, then the soil, the pots,
the window sills, and father's motionless corpse got so caked with bugs
that they too turned complete white, on father's corpse, the web between
his fingers his armpits, the back of his neck all grew completely white, all
of the vines, mother's vine-filled vagina, mother's lips that she used to kiss
father all grew completely white, caked with bugs, and mother scraped
them off
Damu itto, damu itto
Father's corpse called out to mother
The white mealy bugs flew from his mouth

One day, mother stood up
And took out the pruning shears and said,
I'm sick of growing white mealy bugs, I wanted to grow plants, but I've
been growing bugs instead, I wanted to kill them but I've been growing
them instead, maybe what I really intended was to grow them but I've
been killing them instead, these white mealy bugs
Have covered the new shoots
Have covered the backs of leaves
Have covered the spaces between the veins

40

So mother cut off all of those things
The bugs covered the new sprouts that emerged covering new leaves
The bugs covered the spots where the branches separate
The bugs covered the aerial roots
So mother cut off all of those things
Little brother asked, are the plants dead?
Mother said, leave them alone and they'll grow again
And then mother
Stood in front of father's corpse
Took his penis, white with mealy little bugs, in her fingers
And snipped it off
My little brother asked, is it dead?
Mother said, leave it alone and it'll grow again

Mother was covered in gray hair, covered in wrinkles
Father's corpse was silent
It did not yell, did not pucker its face, did not get angry
The penis shriveled up, dry as a bone
Mother picked it up
And said in Japanese,
That wasn't so hard,
Things are easier now,
My shoulders don't get stiff,
My head isn't so heavy any more,
I should have done that ages ago,
Look, what was that thing called again?
You know, the cord that connects the mother to the fetus,
That thing of yours, shut up in a drawer somewhere in Japan?
I didn't think I could get rid of things like that
But it's okay to get rid of those things
I felt bad, those things are important
So I couldn't get rid of things like that
But if I leave it alone, it'll grow again
So it's okay to get rid of things this way
Let's get rid of it, look, like this

Mother said this to us in Japanese
He... is not moving... he... will not get mad
Little brother nudged him and made sure he was not moving
Then began to sing,
"Fudge, fudge, chili pepper, fudge
Mother's got a newborn baby
Wrap it up in tissue paper, send it down the elevator"
We all raised our voices, danced, and jumped
"One floor, two floors, three floors, four floors, five floors, six floors, seven floors,
eight floors,
Then throw it away"
Mother tossed her grey hair and stood up straight
"Fudge, fudge, chili pepper, fudge"
Her wrinkles stretched out and she grew young again
Young enough to have lots more children
"Wrap it up in tissue paper, send it down the elevator"
She took off her clothes, exposing her flabby naked body
"One floor, two floors, three floors, four floors, five floors, six floors, seven floors,
eight floors,
Then throw it away
Yes, throw
It all away"
And we danced
Pieces of the vines and corpse laid on the floor, scattered all over the place

Mother said, I want to see cherry trees, see cherry blossoms
I asked,
Have you ever seen them?
Mother answered,
I have, you've seen it with me, don't you remember?
I answered,
I forgot, I've forgotten completely
Little brother also answered,
I don't remember those things
Mother said,

Let's go see them, let's go home to see them
She was speaking in Japanese,
I don't remember exactly when or where they bloom,
But let's go home, let's go home, and see the cherries in full bloom,
Let's sit under them and eat bento boxes in the breeze,
Let's grind your dried-up umbilical cords into dust and get rid of them

The winds of Santa Ana blew
The winds that blew from the desert
Were strong, hot, and dried up everything, they burned the mountains,
burned the forests
They knocked over trees and clouded the skies with ash
And from the ash-enriched soil
They brought forth new sprouts between the trees
And as the sprouts of the new trees grow over thousands of years
They will become a forest
As the trees grow, they will pass through
Thousands of years of adolescence and
Thousands of years of menopause
And each year they will drop fruit and seedpods with hundreds of seeds
They will drop them one after another onto the ground
And new sprouts will grow

WE LEAVE THE WASTELAND AND GO HOME TO THE RIVERBANK

We thought that after leaving the airport, we needed to buy a bus ticket
And get on the bus and go to another airport
The bus stop was full of people, all rolling big suitcases
The air outside is hot and heavy and humid
We got on the bus and went to another airport, once inside, we walked for
a long time
We went up and down flights of stairs
We got on another airplane, we thought that if we did, we could return to
that town, that place by the riverbank
We got off the airplane and got on a bus, we got off the bus and walked a
long, long way
We thought that was how to get home
We thought we would be going back to that house
Then when we finally reached it
The house was abandoned and overgrown
The roof and walls were crumbling
The grass was overgrown
Behind it was the riverbank
The cherry trees were not in bloom
It was the pomegranates that were blooming
With a red that sunk into the skin
There in the rainy season

As mother walked into the abandoned, overgrown house, she called out,
we're home, we heard the barking of dogs, lots and lots of dogs, we were
frightened out of our wits, little brother let out a cry of fear and started to
run, but mother didn't budge, she fixed her gaze triumphantly on the pack
of dogs and raised her voice, it's me, it's me, and when she did, one of the
big male dogs shook his back and laid down in front of mother, she said,
look, it's Atlas, you remembered me, what a good boy, what a good boy,
and the insanely huge dog started whimpering, covered its ears, and rolled
over on its back, pretending to be powerless, mother rubbed the big male
dog, the dog's penis began to get erect, its penis was bright red, mother

said, come on, let's go, and the dog bounced to its feet, its penis growing longer and longer, the dog intertwined with mother, and mother and the dog bounded into the house with the rest of the pack following behind

The roof and walls were crumbling
The grass was overgrown
Vines in the grass caught at our feet, vines dangled over our heads
As mother tried to slide the door open, the vines that coated it tore away
And the door came out of its track and broke
Grass had grown inside too, creeping across the tatami
The pillars and window frames were covered with vines and mildew
In a teary voice, little brother said,
Oh gross, there's tons of maggots crawling around, what the hell
Little brother and I saw that the house had gone to wrack and ruin
And in it laid the corpse of a man who should have been long gone
The corpse's tongue was moving

The corpse's tongue was moving because of the terrible humidity
Mother embraced it and started crying, I'm so glad that you've stayed alive for us, I missed you, she spoke with sincerity, but it didn't look like it could possibly be alive, little brother asked, who's that? mother said, father, this is your father, I asked, that's our father? the one we abandoned? mother said, not that one, this is the husband I had before, little brother said, this guy also looks like a corpse, mother said, that's because this is the riverbank, everyone who comes to the riverbank turns into a corpse, next to the person she called "father" was the corpse of another dog, mother rubbed the dead dog and said to us, this is Okaasan, she practically raised you, this seemed appropriate since *okaasan* means "mother" in Japanese
We were at the riverbank
I didn't remember seeing any of this
It was the rainy season
Mother said it will rain and rain, but it didn't rain anymore, it didn't rain for several days
Little brother and little sister were nowhere to be seen
I didn't know

What to do with myself there
I didn't know if I should be waiting or looking for something
But there we were so I found the others and went walking around
We kept
Going outside
Wanting to look around
But we could hardly focus our eyes
The bright light outside was filled with green, it was so strong, we couldn't focus
Green grass was growing through even the smallest cracks
There were ferns and moss
There were ferns and moss
There were ferns and moss
The green was so swollen
It looked like it was about to burst
None of this would grow in the wasteland
Where there was no rain, but even if it did somehow manage to grow
As soon as the rain stopped, it would dry up
And die
We walked, the dogs followed
The male dog Atlas, the corpse of Okaasan, the other dogs too
As we walked along the embankment by the river, the different kinds of grass began to droop
Seeds rained down from the spikes at their tips
The tips of the grass cut us
There were a few types of grass we knew in English, horsewood, fleabane, goldenrod
That's all, no more, the rest we didn't know
There was one with tangled heart-shaped leaves that grew even more than the rest
Mother said, this is kudzu
Kuzu? like the word that means "garbage"?
No, *kudzu,* that's its name
The kudzu vines grew and grew
The rainclouds hung down, the wind blew, the different kinds of grass fell

silent and trembled
The wind blew, the various clumps of grass trembled
The trembling traveled across the surface, the entire riverbank shook forward and backward
The clusters of rush attacked the other kinds of grass
The corpses of the other kinds of grass fell before them
The rushes shook in the wind
There were clumps of purple flowers
From a distance, they looked like flecks of gray dust coating the riverbank
There was even some grass that had been so thoroughly gnawed by bugs that it was amazing it was even still alive

Okaasan had given birth to the entire pack of dogs
Dogs decide on their own whose voice they will obey
Dogs also decide who is the head of the household
When this father was alive, he was the head of the household
That's what the dogs had decided
As long as he was the father, it didn't matter what kind of father he was
After he became a corpse, he was still head of the household
Then Okaasan became a corpse too
Even as a corpse, her calling was still to protect children
So she came with us to the riverbank
She did all sorts of things
Lifting children from muddy traps, protecting them from other people or dogs
Even as a corpse, her calling was still to protect children
So she grew agitated and started searching when my little brother and sister were nowhere to be seen
That was because we were at the riverbank
There are corpses at the riverbank
There are any number of them
The riverbank kills every living thing and makes corpses out of them
The riverbank brings back every kind of corpse to life
The grass on the sloped embankment visible from our window was alive
Nothing was visible beyond that

But when we stood on the embankment, we could see
The riverbed that lay beyond
There was more grass growing
Then another embankment
There was another thicket of grass
Beyond where the people walked by and the bicycles ambled across
Growing wildly
The grass was growing wildly
So wildly that it hid everything
The kudzu leaves had turned over
The grass and rushes rustled loudly
A clump of cosmos (one name we knew) had not yet grown to maturity
Their leaves and stems were still growing at a whisper's pace
None of the flowers had grown to maturity yet

Mother said,
There are all kinds of corpses buried there
Mother said,
I've brought all sorts of things there to bury, cats, dogs, mice, fish, turtles, earthworms, grass, stems of plants, inflammable things, non-biodegradable things, I even went out of my way to bury a dead cat there
Mother said,
When you were still little, a cat jumped in front of the car, it got hit and went into spasms, then when it wasn't moving anymore, I brought it back and buried it, a little while later when I tried digging it up again, I couldn't find hide nor hair of it, that's because of the grasses, the grasses eat corpses
Mother said,
If living things come to the riverbank, they get eaten by the grasses and become corpses, sometimes when the rain falls, the water in the river rises up, but when it recedes, it leaves little fish flapping around, sometimes I've returned them to the river, sometimes I've watched them die, sometimes turtles get crushed on the road, sometimes the whole road smells like blood, sometimes frogs get squashed, sometimes snakes, sometimes I have watched them writhe in agony

WE LIVE AT THE RIVERBANK

Mother, who was having so much sex
With the vines inside, left the house and said,
I want to live on the riverbank,
I want to become the riverbank,
I hate living in a house that doesn't let the breeze move through,
It hurts, it itches later, it even makes me swell up,
I don't want to have sex with the vines anymore,
I hate my life of vines and collecting and killing little white mealy bugs,
The wind is blowing hard outside, but the air in the house is completely still,
The white mealy bugs are still everywhere,
The air is so stagnant that the bugs proliferate,
I want to live on the riverbank and become a plant, I want to get rid of the vines,
I only want to take the corpse and the dogs and my kids
That was what mother said, we were the kids
The only way we knew to get by was to tag along with her
So we left home and lived in the middle of the riverbank where the breeze blew through
We wanted to become the riverbank
By "we," I mean Alexa and me and my little brother and little sister
Mother said, the best place to live is the gateball court, no one is there
We can put up a tent, there's water there
We thought yes, we could put up a tent and live there, there's water there
        (And so we went to the riverbank)
Erigeron canadensis and *Conyza sumatrensis* are like twins but
Erigeron canadensis grows old, and *Conyza sumatrensis* blooms
Bugs eat the *Humulus japonicius*
The tips of the *Sorghum halepense* hang heavy with spikes full of seeds
The wind blew
The grasses trembled
The wind blew
The grasses trembled

The entire riverbank swayed back and forth
      (There were many types of grass on the riverbank)
We had an old book about plants
We looked up the names of the grasses
Erigeron canadensis, Conyza sumatrensis,
Caryatia japonica, Humulus japonicius, Sorghum halepense,
Cyperus microiria, Rumex japonicus, Murdannia keisak, Phytolacca americana,
Typha latifolia, Phragmites australis, Miscanthus sacchariflorus, no no,
Typha domingensis, no, Phragmites australis, no no, Miscanthus sacchariflorus,
no
There was a kind of grass whose name we couldn't figure out
It had purple flowers
It grew in clumps all around
It was not in our plant guide
So we could not find the name
Strange
      (We went down onto the embankment)
There was the gateball court
Some old people were playing
The only time they came out was for gateball
Alexa said,
Usually they're hiding underground
One day, an ambulance came
One old man had suddenly stopped moving
He was taken away by the ambulance and disappeared
Two old men stood and watched
The other old folks kept on playing
Alexa said,
Those people will die soon, that's why they don't come even when their
friends die,
They have to play for all they're worth,
That was what she said
But there wasn't anyone there any more
No one came
I don't know when they stopped coming

The gateball court on the riverbank was long forgotten
Before anyone realized
Sorghum halepense had grown wild and taken over
Overgrown
Sorghum halepense,
Erigeron canadensis, Conyza sumatrensis,
Cayratia japonica, Humulus japonicius,
Cyperus microiria, Rumex japonicas, no, Rumex japonicas, Phytolacca americana,
no no,
Typha latifolia, no, Phragmites australis, no no,
Phragmites australis, Miscanthus sacchariflorus, no no no
A small storage shed (there were still things inside)
A faucet (water came out)
A toilet little more than a hole (it had gone dry)
A board leaned up on the toilet (wasps had built a nest)
Mother said, we've got to kill them
An arbor (the bench was rusty)
A barber chair (I spun it with my hands)
Alexa said,
An old man from a barbershop donated it
Alexa said,
Then he died, everyone died, including the old man from the barbershop
We sat little brother and little sister on it and spun it around, they squealed
happily but before long, little brother said he felt sick
I stopped and walked away, but Alexa kept going
Little brother started crying, called her stupid and ugly
Then suddenly he threw up
His vomit traced circles in the air, it got Alexa and me, it stank
Alexa howled, now you've done it, I hope you die
Mother said, oh, you've thrown up, she chuckled and came close
Mother said, this is a good place,
The wind blows through it, there's grass,
The winter is cold, the summer is hot,
The house where we were just now was no good,
The breeze doesn't move through it at all,

It has a roof and walls and little else, I don't understand why it should be so hard to live there,
Open places are better, they feel fresher, they're brighter, look,
We could put a camping tent here, there's water,
There are all kinds of things to eat, poisonous plants too,
Mother said, I want to live here
        (The wind is strong in June)
Mother said, I wish we could live here forever,
Surrounded by the grasses,
I could cut down every last one of those damn vines
A rain cloud flashed in one corner of the sky
Every leaf, every blade of grass flashed with it
Sorghum halepense trembled, *Conyza sumatrensis* trembled
The kudzu leaves fluttered
Sorghum halepense fell over and got back up
Solidago altissima was still young, its stalk and leaves were green
It was pushed over by the wind, as if to say, you, get over there, then it pushed the next stalk
The next stalk too, pushed the next stalk as if to say, you, get over there
The next stalk after the next stalk also pushed the next stalk as if to say, you, get over there, you, get over there,
You, get over there, *Solidago altissima* was pushed over, you, get over there, was pushed, you, get over there
You, get over there
The kudzu vines squirmed, grew up
Onto the embankment, stuck out their tips, waited, then grew tired
The bugs ate holes all through *Humulus japonicus* and *Cayratia japonica* too
Inside the house, the vines
All raised their hands and stood up
        (I want to become part of the riverbank)
        (I want to become part of the riverbank)
A man was seated in the dusk of the arbor, he was older, grimy, shabby, and he was as pale as a corpse, he had a mild case of dementia rather like *Erigeron canadensis*
        (I want to become part of the riverbank)

(Little sister's hands took hold of mine)
Little sister said, a crab bit me
She always says that, a crab bit me, a crab bit me
If I asked her, did a crab really bite you?
She would say, that's right, a crab bit me
So we would give her the third degree, really? a crab bit you?
She would say, a crab, a real crab, it bit me
She would insist and burst out crying, little sister always cries
She did it that time too,
A crab bit our brother
        (I gave him a quick spot check)
He had spots all over his body like he'd been bitten, he was scratching
His eyes were bloodshot, his face and hands had swollen up like balloons
There was a white line on the tip of his nose, it had been there since he was
a baby
A mark from a cup? we'd asked him about it and touched it
When evening came, the line seemed to rise up pale in the darkness
But now his nose was dry
        (He was lying down)
He called out to me,
It itches,
I can't breathe unless I open my mouth,
If I open my mouth, I make a wheezing sound,
It itches, he said through his tears
Mother said, don't scratch, but little brother cried and said, it itches, I've got
to scratch
        (Several days went by with no change)
We said, don't scratch, but he'd scratch, the places he scratched swelled into
blisters full of water
He said through his tears, I didn't scratch it that much, just a little,
Just a little, but the places he scratched still blistered up
Water blisters appeared here and there on his body
Their surfaces were wrinkly and their insides swelled with liquid
        (I want to become part of the riverbank)

Little sister peeped at the blisters

She smiled and said, I see them, I see them

He bent his body into a difficult position, then looked at his blisters then her

And he laughed as he said, look, they're just fat, swollen, ugly little things

In the end, it didn't matter how much he swelled, how bloated he became, how much he wheezed,

They couldn't help themselves, both my little brother and little sister wanted to laugh and play

Both my little brother and my little sister

Both my little brother and my little sister

       (I want to become part of the riverbank)

Erigeron canadensis, Conyza sumatrensis,

Wasteland japonica, Wasteland erigeron, no, humulus, Wasteland, no, sorghum,

Wasteland cyperus, Wasteland rumex, Wasteland americana,

Wasteland phytolacca americana, Typha domingensis, Typha orientalis, Wasteland typha,

No, Phragmites australis, no, Phragmites australis, Phragmites australis, Phragmites australis,

Conyza miscanthus, no, Miscanthus sacchariflorus, Wasteland miscanthus, Long ago, no, Wasteland, no, Riverbank, no, Miscanthus sacchariflorus

The *no no* kudzu vines grew *no no* noticeably over them, they climbed onto the embankment

Stuck out their tips ever so *no no* noticeably, and waited, then grew tired

The bugs ate holes through the *Wasteland japonicus* and the *Thicket japonicus* too,

Even the vines, inside, the house, *no no, no,*

Slid out, *no*, of mother's vagina

Put up both hands, *no*, and all stood up together

       (I want to become part of the riverbank)

Little brother was eaten up

He was so eaten and swollen up that he hardly seemed like my brother any more

In desperation, mother flopped down on the tatami in the house, opened her mouth, wheezed

And cried

And cried

Little brother called out to me, it itches, it itches

Alexa got angry and shouted,

Shut up,

Shut up, I don't wanna hear your stupid voice

      (I want to become a plant that grows vines)

      (I want to become a plant that grows spikes full of seed)

I cut all my fingernails short and washed my hands

And I scratched little brother's body lightly

I scratched him lightly, lightly

I scratched him lightly, but his skin grew raw, and liquid began seeping out

Mother said, all living things get eaten by mosquitoes

The difference has to do with whether you're allergic to mosquito spit or not

And whether you dwell on the itchiness or not

We all have the same invisible bite marks

On our bodies as well

On my body, on Alexa's body

On little sister's body

On little brother's body, which had transformed so terribly

There were bite marks all over

Everybody got eaten

All of us were eaten up

      (I want to be naturalized)

      (I want to be naturalized)

We were eaten up

ON THE RIVERBANK

The different types of grass on the riverbank shook their seed pods, they propagated there, filling the whole place, whether we knew their names or not, the grasses growing in the wasteland bloomed with yellow flowers, but the flowers quickly wilted and became red, the clusters of rushes on the riverbank still had not gone into heat, meanwhile hard, pale spikes of seed trembled at their tips, the tall rushes brandished their saw-like leaves as we passed by, when they cut our skin and the blood seeped out, the rushes let out a sigh and started acting as if they realized what they had done, meanwhile, they stuck out their tongues and licked our blood from their leaves, the kudzu vines crawled up the slopes of the embankment, they grew as far as the path on top of the embankment, they groped about at random, they touched us too, sometimes they could not completely control their lust and let out a stifled little laugh, the water was completely red at the edge, the shellfish had laid their eggs and they looked like bloody froth, the riverbank and the walls of mud and the bases of the rushes and the abandoned car were all completely red, the vines that mother was growing inside the house crawled outside like the other plants, and in the middle of all of it, father's corpse sat peacefully

ON THE RIVERBANK

Erigeron canadensis, Conyza sumatrensis,
Sorghum halepense, Great wasteland japonica, Asteraceae, Wasteland princess, no,
Humulus, Cayratia, Boehmeria nivea, Wasteland, no, Barbarian, Great, Princess,
Sorghum,
Wasteland cyperus microiria, Wasteland rumex japonicus, Wasteland erigeron,
Erigeron annuus, Erechtites hieracifolia, Bidens frondosa,
Paederia scandens, scan, scan, scandalous,
No, Wasteland, no, Phytolacca americana princess, Wasteland americana princess,
Typha latifolia, oh, Tyhpa latifolia, Wasteland, no, Typha latifolia,
No, Phragmites australis, no, Miscanthus sacchariflorus, Phragmites australis,
Miscanthus sacchariflorus, Phragmites australis, Miscanthus sacchariflorus,
Farting, vomiting, shitting, stinging vines,
Princess, Long ago, Erigeron, oh, Wasteland, no, Asteraceae

MEMORIES

I wondered if a corpse was all father had ever really been
I seemed to remember any number of fathers in our home
I seemed to remember the father we abandoned in the wasteland with Santa Ana
I felt like there had been many others too
I said, I seem to remember, Alexa said, me too, me too
We tried asking mother, what about back then?,
It seemed like there were any number of fathers before this one
She said, you must be imagining things,
Do mean Yoshioka? Or Tom?,
But I can't imagine you'd be able to remember them,
Yoshioka and Tom
Someone had held me as I slept, my face buried in his pillow
Meanwhile I kept thinking, *ewww*, he stinks, *ewww*, he stinks
I wondered, which father was that?
Alexa also chimed in, yes, he stunk, he stunk
No, that wasn't our father now, that wasn't the father who died either, he stunk much more than that, one day he suddenly disappeared, and another father came and took his place
Alexa chimed in, I remember, I remember
He slipped away like a cat, there were others who disappeared but are still here even despite disappearing, there were others that just turned into corpses

One father had a shiny rifle, that was about the time Okaasan came, she was a good, purebred dog, but she was not a hunting dog, she was a herding dog, that father trained her to fetch even though she was a herder, and he went out hunting with her, she brought back dead ducks that had been blown to bits, if a purebred herding dog bites down on the corpse of a duck, there is no way it'll let go, Okaasan was no good as a hunting dog but she still had potential as a herder, she would protect the children from other people and other dogs, she bit other people and dogs, she would go with us to the riverbank every time we went, when one of us would go

away, she would bide her time and count us, one two three four, one two
three four

One two three four, one two three four
Until we all were there
Even after we were all there, she bided her time
As if she weren't still counting
One two three four, one two three four
Right then, right there, Alexa and I
Buried the dead duck that father had brought back, blown to bits
But that father also disappeared suddenly like a cat sneaking off

WE MAKE OUR WAY IN

At the roots of the different types of grass
The corpses were buried
Lots of corpses were buried
Corpses of grass and corpses of animals
We made a hideout on the riverbank where the corpses were buried
Imagined downfall, countless corpses, the desire to live and grow
We put all those powers into practice there
We stepped over the corpses of the grass
And got caught in the mud
Little brother and little sister got caught in it, Alexa and I did too, we got
so thoroughly caught in it that we couldn't get out, each time one of us
got caught, Okaasan found herself stumped and paced around, she licked
the fretting child all over, her tongue was incredibly hot for a corpse, we
grabbed onto her tongue and the fur at the back of her neck and finally
escaped, when Alexa got caught, once again Okaasan paced around and
licked her all over, Alexa grabbed something in the mud, but it was cold and
squishy, she screamed *yuck!* it was a corpse, the corpse of a big cat, it came
sliding out, *yuck!* everyone got all worked up, Alexa screamed, little sister
jumped back, *barf! barf!* little brother danced around as he cried, Okaasan
and Atlas had turned upside down and were on their backs, rubbing their
backs on the corpse with wild abandon, *yuck! yuck! yuck! yuck! yuck!*
Yuck, I say!
Alexa said, I'm never going back to the riverbank again
But in the end we did go back
We went back to the riverbank and climbed down the embankment
We played around, pulling out the living things, spinning them around,
putting them in our mouths
We found nests of birds, dens of tanuki, and lots more corpses
We stepped in them and touched them
There were so many corpses on the riverbank
Of cats and rats and fishes and frogs and birds and bugs
Ones that were all rotten and looked sort of like human babies
We liked looking at them and poking them

I couldn't tell if we liked the corpses or hated them
None of us could tell
But we wanted to look at them
We really wanted to look at them
We didn't have the power to do anything, no power at all
To do anything to rotten, slimy animals like that
We, who were looking at it, were alive, we were incredibly strong and big
There were so many different kinds of corpses
It was because of the grass
It caught and consumed every creature it could
Anything that died on the riverbank became a corpse
It didn't matter if you were alive or dead
If you came to the riverbank, the grasses would eat you, and you would
become a corpse
I wanted to bury Okaasan on the riverbank sometime
Dig a shallow hole in the grass on the riverbank and bury her
The grass on the riverbank would swallow her in no time
That's probably what Okaasan wanted as well

We went down the embankment into the thick growth on the riverbank
Little brother said, you'll get bitten by bugs so don't follow me, but we
always did anyway
If little brother was there, little sister would be there too
He threatened her, I won't carry you if you can't walk,
I'll leave you behind if you ask me to carry you,
But she made a serious face and did her best to walk, she came so Okaasan
followed along too, Okaasan came so Atlas followed along too, Atlas came
so the other dogs followed along too
It was a muddy mess below the embankment
There were cattails
There were thick spikes at the top
Little brother said, they look like poop, like poop
Little sister yelled, they look like poop, like poop
There were cattails that were thicker than any poop
The dead stalks had fallen over

The new stalks had started coming up in between
If we didn't step on the dead cattails, we'd get stuck in the mud

The man came out in the evenings, he came out in the evenings and sat under the arbor, the man was older and looked ratty, he was as pale as a corpse, he had a mild case of dementia rather like *Erigeron canadensis*, he came in the evening and did weird things, I saw him, Alexa did too, something really weird, Alexa said, *gross*, he's as faded and worn out as *Senecio vulgaris*
Mother said, a long time ago, the riverbank was a field of nothing but cattails, but the river used to flood so much that one time, they dug up the field of cattails, ripped them out by the roots, and made a pond, she said that was when they made the gateball court, the tennis courts, the embankment, and the walking path, they made lawns and built arbors here and there, that really took me aback, suddenly there were buildings there in the middle of the riverbank, still, that was a long time ago, now there's always someone sleeping under each of the arbors, caretakers used to come pretty often, but no one comes anymore, there's no more lawn grass, most of the walking path is overgrown, the whole riverbank is endlessly overgrown, the cattails have grown tall and thick, they grow on top the embankment too, mother said, there was a man that hid in the thick overgrowth, early one morning he abducted a girl, and ever since then, they come and cut down the grasses periodically
Even though it doesn't do any good
Cut them and they'll just grow back right away
They grow back right away
They grow back right away
The first ones they cut are *Sorghum halepense*
Conyza sumatrensis and *Erigeron canadensis*
It's unfortunate they all look so similar you can't tell them apart
You think it's *Conyza sumatrensis*, and it's *Erigeron canadensis*
You think it's *Erigeron canadensis*, and it's *Conyza sumatrensis*
They grow back right away
They grow back right away
The regular old mugwort

Grows and gets old
The kudzu grows long creeping tendrils
It covers the grass, covers the telephone poles
It grows leaves and shakes in the wind
It wraps around little girls' ankles
And turns over
And laughs
And shakes
It shakes and propagates until the entire riverbank is swaying backwards and forwards
In those days, I could only see a single star
There might have been more, but we only remember one
It was always visible in the southern sky
It was humid, but the wind cleared the air
The clouds moved, sometimes they'd shine with a burst of light, maybe they were storm clouds
We played outside until the stars came out
The darkness came and we couldn't see the grass anymore
Only white things rose out of the darkness—white flowers, scrap paper, white shoes
The night herons took off in flight
There were ducks and bats in the sky
Everything was flying around at that hour
Something flickered near the water's edge
That was where the cooking pits were
There were tall chimneys
Some days there was smoke, sometimes not
Leftover bones were scattered on the riverbank, human shapes would flicker there like flames
They were talking about it in a place called "school"
Right then, on the dark riverbank
As we were looking at the flickering thing
Alexa said,
Oh, look, a human finger
My little brother immediately burst into tears,

Huh, where? where?,
Stupid! you promised you wouldn't say stuff like that any more
He got up and ran away
Alexa said, you're in a bad mood
Making little brother cry
Making little sister cry

Little sister drew pictures, always the same picture, a picture of our house, but then, Alexa started laughing and said, your house looks just like the cooking pit, there were four people in the family, they were standing, smiling in front of a red house with a roof and chimney, father, mother, little brother, and I, but Alexa was nowhere to be seen, mother, little brother, and I were smiling, we all had long arms and legs like spiders, only one of us was lying on our sides and smiling, that was father, that is the corpse of the father that mother had so carefully drug around, my little sister couldn't draw the corpse very well, but it was there, lying down, smiling, with arms and legs like a spider's
We didn't know which of the fathers it was, we didn't know which of the fathers was my little sister's father, we didn't know which of the fathers my little sister remembered
She grinned,
That's our family
Alexa pointed to the cooking pit and began to sing,
Burned to death in the cooking pit,
Bones and pants, all burnt smooth,
Flames licking their bottoms,
Put on the pretty pants left behind,
And now go live there, stupid,
And don't come back, scum
Little sister didn't understand, but she started crying and screaming
Until all that came out were hiccupping sounds
That's our family

There were all sorts of things near the cooking pits
Something-something treatment plant (we couldn't read the characters

something, something)
Crematorium for cats and dogs
Alexa said, that's where they melt dead babies,
Someone was talking about it in a place called "school,"
They said it stinks so bad you can hardly stand it,
No one knows about the riverbank or the corpses so that's why they say such things,
Everyone says that, they laughed at the riverbank,
They laughed at us,
They made fun of us
There were all sorts of things near the cooking pits
Something-something treatment plant (we couldn't read the characters *something, something*)
Crematorium for cats and dogs
The place for melting dead babies
Unwanted babies die on their own, so you can just take them there and melt them down
They melt the dead babies there and let them go in the river
They collect the corpses of the cats and dogs
Until the crematorium is full and then they burn them all at once
Right there on the spot, they throw out the ones that won't fit
That's why the riverbank stinks so bad, that's what someone said, and everyone laughed
It stinks, it stinks, they said, and everyone laughed
(I remembered the bad passport
I remembered the way we were left behind in that huge, empty airport hallway
That huge, empty airport hallway)
Everyone just wants power
The power to make people sad or frightened
The power to make them cry or stop crying
I hate it, I hate it
I wish there was no such power
We'd be just fine if there was no such thing
As the power to make people do what you want

But when we went back home
We were the only ones on the riverbank
They collect the corpses of the cats and dogs
Until the crematorium is full and then they burn them all at once
Right there on the spot, they throw out the ones that won't fit
Alexa said, look, the corpse of a dog, you're stepping on it
Little brother cried
Little sister sobbed
It's fun to tease them and make them cry
It's more fun to make someone cry than to be the one who's crying
I just said we'd be just fine without power
But what would that be like?
All right, I won't do it anymore

ON THE RIVERBANK

The man we'd seen at the riverbank came out in the evenings, he was there at the riverbank at the same time each evening, he came out in the evenings and sat under an arbor, no one else was there, the man was older, grimy, and kind of ratty, as pale as a corpse, as tall as *Conyza sumatrensis*, he came there in the evenings and did the same thing, he took out his penis and touched it, as he touched it, he'd twitch a little, the penis would rise up, we'd smell something we'd thought we'd smelled before somewhere, his penis got shiny in his hands, white stuff flew out, then the smell went away, the man came out at the same time to the same arbor, he grabbed his penis and twitched in the same way, we smelled the same smell, and then it went away, when evening fell, we went to watch, we'd watch from a distance so we wouldn't be discovered, then we'd go home

MICHIYUKI

By late summer, everyone on the riverbank was dead
Not just the creatures, but the summer grass, the rusted bicycles, the
summer grass
Cars without doors or windows, the warped porn magazines, the summer
grass
Empty cans with food stuck inside and empty bottles full of muddy water
Girl's panties and condoms, father's corpse, and so much summer grass

The riverbank only meant to control you
The summer grass touched our bodies
The seeds fell down onto our bodies
On the bank, I noticed a kind of grass that multiplied conspicuously
It was about one meter high and looks like some kind of rice
It had spikes full of seed
It was everywhere
It glimmered white in the dim evening light
Sticky liquid oozed from the spikes full of seed
The dogs got sticky
The dogs smelled terrible
The dogs agonized and rubbed their bodies onto the ground
The man from the riverbank appeared in the evening
Every evening he appeared and sat under an arbor
Completely alone
Older, grimy, shabby, pale as a corpse
When his penis rose up
A smell rose up like the one from the rice-like grass on the bank
The penis in his hand glistened and glistened

The flowers of the kudzu also rose up, I noticed the kudzu flowers rising
up here and there, one day, we became tangled in the tendrils of the kudzu
plants, I heard something slithering along abruptly, no sooner had I heard
this than a tendril trapped my heel, it hit me, and knocked me on my back
into a bush, there *Sorghum halepense* rattled in the wind, the unfamiliar grass
from before started shaking, releasing its scent, then the tendril stretched all

the further, crawling onto my body, getting into my panties, and creeping into my vagina, I inhaled and exhaled, I exhaled and the tendril slid in, I inhaled and the tendril slid out, I exhaled again and it slid further in, my body was turned this way and that like the leaves of the kudzu, my body opened and closed over and over, and Alexa watched all of this, Alexa was watching, watching and laughing, I became angry, so angry, I got up and shoved Alexa away, she fell down on her back, the tendrils clung to Alexa too, Alexa also turned this way and that, the tendril also went inside her vagina, deep inside, and she started to cry

Everyone was dead
Father
Little brother
Mother and me

Ahh… think I'll, I'll think to myself
Pack it in
And buy a pick-up
Take it down to L.A.
Find a place
To call my own
Maybe that place would be a hot spring
One that heals eczema, dermatitis, neuralgia
Menopausal disorders, diabetes, infectious diseases
A hot spring among hot springs, one that would fix you up right away
A place where you could soak yourself, open your pores, scrub your body, swell up
A place where you will want to live again and *start a brand new day*

Little brother cried, hey, I'm itchy, so itchy, I told him not to scratch, but he did it anyway, the place he scratched soon turned into a blister, little brother cried, I didn't scratch it that much, only a little, but even so, the place he scratched turned into a blister, there were blisters all over his body, after they ruptured, they got inflamed and full of pus
Little brother no longer seemed like himself, he was horribly swollen, he

rolled all over the house, mouth open, wheezing, crying
And crying

Mother said, I want to take him to a hot spring, I've heard of a hot spring that's good for your skin, why don't we take your dead father and dead dog along too to soak in the water, so we decided to go, we just left everything as it was, we left the leftover food, dirty clothes, and wet towels just as they were, then we carefully laid my wheezing brother on the rear seat, and we stuffed some other things in the car, my little sister, spare clothes, the corpses, the dogs, plastic bags, pillows, food and drink (even some flowerpots), so much stuff, then we took off, I stared at the road from the passenger seat and asked, how do we get there? from the driver's seat, mother answered, it's over that mountain

Mother said, that hot spring
Will fix you up right away,
Soak yourself, open your pores, scrub your body, swell up,
It'll heal your eczema, your blisters,
Your skin infections, your ringworm,
Your dermatitis, your infectious diseases,
Your atopy, your allergies,
Your corpses, your impending death, your having died, and even death in general
A hot spring that will fix you up you right up right away,
A place where you will want to live again and start a brand new day,
Anyway, mother said,
Let's go over that mountain
The back seat was full, no space left for your feet
The car was old and rickety, and there hadn't been much foot room from the start
But still we stuffed it full
With things, with garbage, with food
With people, with dogs, and with corpses
Until there was no space left
It stunk of dogs

It stunk of death
Little brother was wheezing in the back seat
Little sister sometimes cried out as if she'd just remembered something
She said, I left something back at home,
She said, please go back, I forgot something
But we can't go back
Someone asked, if we just keep going
Through the fork in the road,
Won't that be Toroku?,
Won't that be Kurokami?,
Won't that be Kokai?,
The Jōgyōji crossing,
Through Uchi-tsuboi,
Up Setozaka slope,
Shouldn't we go
All the way over there?
She knew the way to the big camphor tree where that samurai-monk was buried
At the samurai-monk's big tree, we turned right at a three-way intersection
We could see the huge treetop of the samurai-monk's big camphor tree
From where we were, it looked so huge
That I bet it'd block out the whole universe if you were standing underneath
There was a path for tractors and pick-ups right there
We turned right at the three-way intersection
There was a small stone bridge, we crossed it
Then came out at another three-way intersection
We went straight
We went straight
We went up the road
We went through tangerine orchards on both sides, and when we came out
We were on mountainous roads
Where it was dark even in the middle of the day
The road meandered through a forest with shining leaves
The road meandered
The road drew close to a cliff

Then moved away
Ahh… I think to myself
Think I'll pack it in, and buy a pick-up, take it down to L.A.
Mother started to sing in a key way too high for her,
Ahh… Think I'll…
A tangle of karasuuri flowers and fruits
Ahh, Think I'll…
A thick bunch of worm-eaten leaves
A scarlet flower was blooming, probably a garden species that escaped somebody's yard
In the shade of the other plants, a large white flower was blooming
A flower pale and white
It couldn't have been a garden species, it was pale because it was in the shade
Another car came
We passed each other
We guessed the car was going home from the hot spring
All fixed up, the driver had fixed his skin trouble and was going home
I tried to get a good look
But the car sped by us in a flash
Much further and we'd be at the seashore
The seashore facing west
Mother said, doesn't look like there is a hot spring, beyond this is the Pure Land
The dog noticed the smell of the sea
It stuck its nose out the window, howling for the sea
Mother said, we should've crossed a large bridge,
I forgot the name, but it's a large bridge,
There were big floods here in the late nineteenth and the mid-twentieth centuries,
Lots of earth, sand, and drowned bodies got caught on the bridge,
But the floods downstream were even worse,
We screwed up when we missed the bridge,
The only water we've seen has been those small streams,
Mother said, we've definitely gone the wrong way,

Mother said, we'll never get there if we keep going this way
The dog that was howling for the sea rose up in the back seat
And walked across little brother
Alexa shouted in anger
Mother said, we'd better start all over,
I give up
Little brother cried out in a high voice,
You can't give up,
Is that all you know how to do?
Alexa shouted, shut up
Little sister wept, I told you, I told you
The dog barked
Lots of dogs barked
Alexa shouted, I can't take it anymore, I can't, I can't
She said, no one ever listens to me
She sunk her face into her thighs, curled up, and started to sob
Her voice grew louder, more childish than little brother's
More infantile than little sister's
She cried on and on, on and on
Only sobbing
On and on
On and on
Mother said, we should've turned around,
But if we did, we'd just get more lost,
Let's keep going down the hill to the sea, then go home round the cape
So that's how we got back home
Nothing fixed
Nothing found
Nothing
We failed
It was no good
It was all over

SONG

Think I'll pack it in
And buy a pick-up
Take it down to L.A.
Find a place to call my own
And try to fix up
Start a brand new day

From Neil Young, "Out on the Weekend"

SONG

This is a song I learned long ago
When I was living in the wasteland that smelled of sage
I sang it
With my little brother
"Fudge, fudge, chili pepper, fudge
Mother's got a newborn baby
Wrap it up in tissue paper
Send it down the elevator
One floor, two floors, three floors, four floors, five floors, six floors, seven floors,
eight floors,
Then throw it away"

Want me to sing it again?

"Fudge, fudge, chili pepper, fudge
Mother's got a newborn baby
Wrap it up in tissue paper
Send it down the elevator
One floor, two floors, three floors, four floors, five floors, six floors, seven floors,
eight floors,
Then throw it away"

SEPTEMBER —TH

"Mother Arrested, Children Armed and Standing Their Ground (September –th)"

"On the –th of this month, the Sado office of the K prefectural police received reports of child endangerment and abuse. Upon carrying out a search of a private home in Sado township, several dead bodies were discovered in a mummified state. One body appears to be that of of H-tō J-shi (aged 49). H-tō's wife, I-mi (aged 46) is being treated as a suspect in the case, and was detained for questioning, but when police attempted to take her children into safekeeping, the children let loose their dogs, set fires in the surrounding area, shot off firearms, and stood their ground inside the house. A couple of years ago, the entire H-tō household returned from living abroad and began illegally squatting in the home located along the Sado River. The family had several dogs, but it is said that the majority of the animals had gone feral and were causing problems in the neighborhood. It appears that the firearms were hunting rifles that J-shi had used for hunting. It is unclear how many children there are, and their ages and genders are unknown. Because the main priority is keeping the children safe, the Sado police have chosen to keep a close eye on the situation instead of using force. Meanwhile, they are carefully trying to convince the children to stand down."

KAWARA NATSUKUSA, OR SUMMER GRASS
ON THE RIVERBANK

The summer grass grew, the ivy grew tangled
The sealed-up car stayed there all summer
The summer grass grew, the ivy grew tangled
Cars are often abandoned
The summer grass grew, the ivy grew tangled
Nobody did a thing and meanwhile
The summer grass grew, the ivy grew tangled
The car gradually grew larger
One day, there was a loud sound, the seals on the car burst off, the doors
opened
Four bodies had been fermenting inside
Their last wills and testaments, their belongings, their driver's licenses had
all grown bloated
The policemen wore masks as if the car was full of poison gas
I watched them carry away the corpses
The summer grass grew, the ivy grew tangled
The weather was bad all summer, suddenly it grew hot
The summer grass grew, the ivy grew tangled
People came and mowed the embankment
As it was cut, *Sorghum halepense* rustled back and forth, back and forth
It cried, why don't you help me? I'm your friend, we played so much on the
embankment
But everyone was killed
Everyone, everything was killed
The embankment was suffocating with the smell of the blood of the grass
We walked among the wreckage
The blood of the grass dirtied little brother's hands
The blood of the grass dirtied little sister's hands too
The corpses had been collected and piled high
A week later, a new batch of *Sorghum halepense* had already grown knee
high
Two weeks later, it had grown as high as a person
The pile of corpses dried out and changed color

The wind was amazing, beginning in one corner of the sky, the rainclouds began to glisten, every leaf, every single leaf shimmered green as if lit from the inside, it was blinding in every direction, I could hear something, the sound went on incessantly, it was the sound of the wind rustling in the different types of grass, *Sorghum halepense* raised a fuss, *Solidago altissima* made a fuss, its had completely turned yellow at the tips, the kudzu leaves wriggled about, the wind massaged and stroked the clusters of *Sorghum halepense*, the stalks of *Sorghum halepense* fell over one after another then bounded back up, then the kudzu crawled on top, it crawled on top of *Solidago altissima*, it crawled on top of *Sorghum halepense*, it crawled out onto the path at the top of the embankment, I could hear someone's voice, it came bursting up to where I was, but I couldn't hear Alexa's voice, the dogs barked, they barked a lot, but I couldn't hear Alexa's voice, I was inside a clump of *Solidago altissima*, it was completely yellow, then the different clumps of grass began to shake back and forth, the grass in front of me had been eaten by bugs, it was full of holes, I could hear someone's voice, it came bursting up to where I was, but I could not hear Alexa's voice, the dogs barked, they barked a lot, I was inside a clump of *Solidago altissima*, then something pushed me, told me to go over there, it was *Solidago altissima* calling out and telling me to get out of there, so I went even deeper into the riverbank where there was no *Sorghum halepense* or *Solidago altissima*, the only thing there was the grass with the purple flower and the name that I didn't know, it was gathered in clusters, but all of it was dead

KAWARA ALEXA, OR WILD GRASS ON THE RIVERBANK

Alexa screamed, everybody get in the house, then she let the dogs out one after the other, the dogs barked angrily in terrifying voices as they ran, Okaasan flew through the air at full pace and clamped her jaws down on the man in front, the man that Okaasan bit let out a long, long scream, Okaasan dangled from the man's arm in midair, the man struck Okaasan's body with something that looked like a stick, and I watched Okaasan fall heavily to the ground and collapse

Right then, Alexa brought something out of the house
It was the hunting rifle father had used to shoot ducks a long time ago
Alexa put in the bullets in like everything was completely normal, like she was changing a battery
She braced herself, aimed, and fell back
There was a loud noise
Alexa's face was covered with pimples
Pimples
Her forehead, her cheeks, the tip of her nose
The back of her neck, the side of her nose, above her upper lip
She looked completely different than when little brother was eaten by bugs
She was erupting from the inside
She stunk
Of human oil, human hatefulness, human ill will
Alexa fell back
It became silent for a second, everyone stopped moving
Then everybody let up a shout simultaneously
I went into the house and Alexa, who had fallen back, shouted

The top of the embankment suddenly went up in flames
There were piles of grass that had been killed and had dried up
Flames shot up and spread over the entire surface of the dry, dead riverbank
Little brother started screaming and ran
Alexa stood up slowly
I slipped into *Solidago altissima*

Alexa was watching me as I slipped in
The grass before my eyes had been eaten by bugs, it was full of holes
I kept walking
Alexa was watching me
The ground grew wet and full of cattails, the cattails were really tall, lots and lots of them were standing there with stalks on them that looked like poop, lots and lots of the old cattails had died and fallen over, I walked across the corpses of the cattails, before long the different kinds of miscanthus began gathering together, they were different from the friendly *Sorghum halepense* and *Solidago altissima* on top of the embankment, the miscanthus wanted to cut into me with the edges of its leaves, I got covered in blood, the grass with the purple flower whose name I didn't know also formed big clumps here, but all of the clumps had dried up and died
My face stung, the miscanthus stuck me all over, my face and body both itched, I closed my eyes, I know my little brother was crying, if I only had him there, I would have put my arms around his shoulders and walked away with him, but I was alone and there was nothing I could do about that
The dogs barked, stopped, barked, then stopped again, they were far away, the birds and the bugs and the frogs were all really noisy, I closed my eyes and squatted on the ground

The dogs barked, stopped, barked, then stopped again
I couldn't make out Okaasan's bark
The dogs barked, stopped, barked, then stopped again
I could make out Atlas's bark
I couldn't make out Okaasan's bark
The dogs barked, stopped, barked, then stopped again

"Your little brother is crying somewhere, we went to look for him, we were in someone's apartment building, the staircase twisted about in complicated ways, and we couldn't get to apartment 504, at last we found someone who could speak the language we spoke in the wasteland, you're really lucky, he said"
Was I dreaming?
I opened my eyes, I felt like I was looking for something, had I been

dreaming?

I opened my eyes, I felt like I hadn't slept, I felt like I'd been awake the whole time, looking for something

I realized that everything was the same as when I lay down

I lost hope

Then I had another dream

"Your little brother has turned into a lump of flesh, when we saw that we looked for a refrigerator to put him in, but we left the refrigerator at our old house, so we realized we had to get back there, back to the old house"

Every time I opened my eyes, I lost hope, then I fell asleep again

But once again I woke up, then lost hope again

Alexa should have been having the same dream, she should have lost hope too

Alexa was me

The wild grass was me

I was Alexa

I was the wild grass

We were exactly alike, just like *Erigeron canadensis* and *Conyza sumatrensis*

Some people who knew that we wanted to become part of the riverbank came and looked at us, they looked at my brother's swollen body and held their breath, they made accusations against our mother who wanted to become part of the riverbank too, then even more people came, they found father's corpse, they took mother away, they found even more corpses, lots of people came to catch us, the dogs attacked, brother set the grass on fire, and the riverbank burned, Okaasan turned into a corpse, Alexa fired a gun and everyone stood still, little brother was probably still whining to me, I'm itchy

Alexa would probably have said in an angry voice, go to bed, it'll be fine

Brother would have no doubt closed his eyes and immediately said, it itches

Alexa would probably have said, go to bed, it'll be fine

They would probably have repeated that same conversation over and over again

Alexa had seen everything from beginning to end

"A big man is trying to open the door with his big hands, a big, heavy door that

spins round and round, like the kind that you'd see in a submarine"
I opened my eyes, it must have been another dream
The man's voice got louder, unnaturally loud
It was an unnatural voice, he was using a machine to make it louder
The dogs barked and barked, stopped, barked, then stopped again
We couldn't hear Okaasan's bark, the dogs barked, stopped
A man said, *you must...*
A man said, *when you come...*
A woman said, *please...*
I was crying and babbling, I couldn't understand what they were saying
A woman said, *...right?* then the volume went up, and there was a loud,
mechanical squeal
Then a man said, *don't you...?*
...xa
...grass
The man was calling out to me
There's nothing more you can do
Silence
You're being stupid
You're really stupid
You're behaving stupidly, like monkeys or some dumb octopus
You're hopeless, like some dumb octopus, nothing more we can do
And then there was another loud, mechanical squeal, the dogs barked and
barked, stopped, barked, then stopped again

I was covered in mud, my body itched all over, my face and my hands
and the back of my throat burned, the cattail spikes that looked like poop
hanging in the air fell over one after another, scattered, and disappeared,
as they were scattering and disappearing in the air above me, I grabbed
them and pressed them to my face, I pressed them to my burning, irritated
face, the fuzz got in my nose, the fuzz stuck to the bottom of my chin, the
grass that had sticky seed stalks was shaking along the water's edge, the
miscanthus made a rustling noise, but this grass didn't make any sound, it
let off a sickly sweet scent, I wanted to know its name but I didn't, it made
me nervous, I wanted to know its name, I wanted to say it

Sorghum halepense
Erigeron canadensis
Solidago altissima
I tried saying those names over and over, those were the names I knew, but I still didn't know the name of that other grass I didn't know, the dogs barked, stopped, barked, then stopped again, they were far away, the birds and the bugs and the frogs were loud, I closed my eyes and kept them closed, I thought I ought to keep them closed forever, I was the only one who thought that, not the two of us, until yesterday, Alexa and I were just like *Erigeron canadensis* and *Conyza sumatrensis*, but now I am completely alone here

"Fudge, fudge, chili pepper, fudge
Mother's got a newborn baby
Wrap it up in tissue paper
Send it down the elevator
One floor, two floors
Three floors, four floors
Five floors, six floors
Seven floors, eight floors"
I sang this as I walked through the wasteland that smelled of sage
Sometimes I found a dead rabbit or lizard
The creatures there all smelled of sage
They could die over and over again, and still they didn't die completely
"I was standing next to my sleeping father, he was sleeping but wasn't dead, I took his hand, and it snapped right off, breast milk started gushing out, I hoped he'd come back to life, I shouted in a loud voice, 'mother, mother, father broke,' that's when she flew out the window to where I was, she said, oh, my goodness, he's broken, and with that, his body withered and began to shrink"
Was I dreaming again?
I stood up and began walking, I walked to the edge of the river, I almost stepped on the corpse of a cat, water had collected and formed a big pond, on the banks of the pond was one of the arbors, every time the rain fell, the water would overflow and this place would be covered in water, then the water would withdraw and the grass would grow again, it would grow

really dense and thick, I sat down under the arbor and watched the pond, ripples spread across the surface, everything reflected on it trembled, a kind of grass whose name I didn't know grew around the pond and put out white spikes full of seeds, its reflection trembled in the pond, then I heard someone's voice and the man from the riverbank appeared, he was muttering something as he wiped the soles of his shoes on the grass, then everything was quiet, he sat down and watched the ripples on the pond, before long the breeze stopped and the ripples disappeared, the man got up and walked briskly to the water's edge and threw a stone into the water, it created big rings that extended all the way across the surface of the pond
The man from the riverbank started talking to me, why is it that it's so much more interesting to watch the trees and grass and lights reflected in the water than looking at the real thing, the man from the riverbank didn't think he knew me, but I knew him so he must have known who I was, I had never smelled anything like him, all of my fathers had stunk, but they were not as stinky as he was, the man had a strange smell, one that threatened to burn my nose, yet it was sickly sweet, and I wanted to smell it some more
I asked, did you step on the corpses?
He said, I stepped on them on purpose,
He said, there are lots of them, lots of corpses on the riverbank,
Because everything turns into a corpse
I said, Alexa once said she'd like to find a person's corpse,
I bet that'd be really scary

It probably would be scary
Why? Why would it be scary?
Because they are completely different than us
Because some part of you thinks they might come back to life
Because they might come back to life
And transform into something else
Or maybe it is just the way they are that is so scary
The way they transform into something else
Mother, help me!
But even if I called out to her, she'd probably just wave a dried-out arm at me

Little brother was scratching himself all over
I had to take charge and get out of there

The man said, that'd be scary, really scary
He said, there's a railway crossing over there, one time someone committed suicide by throwing himself in front of a train there, I was crossing the tracks when I realized what had happened, someone had cleaned it up but there were countless little fragments of flesh they couldn't get to, it was like someone had sprinkled the whole place with little bits of meat, they were under the track and under the gravel, the body had transformed from the way it was
I said, Alexa once said she'd like to find a person's corpse,
She said we could probably find one on the riverbank,
She wanted to find one, finding one would probably give us goose bumps
The man from the riverbank took out his penis, got into a kneeling position on the bench, and began rubbing it, when I looked at him, he told me that he didn't care, he said, you were watching, weren't you? you saw me do this, I was watching you too
I said, Alexa said that's gross
His penis grew bigger, but the man from the riverbank kept on rubbing
He said, you probably think I'm stupid
I said, Alexa, me and the others said that's gross

The man from the riverbank patiently rubbed his penis, and as he kneeled in his strange position and rubbed it, he spoke to me for a long, long time about the corpses and the plants on the riverbank
He said, when I was little, I liked the story about how the rabbit was on the verge of death but was healed by the seed spike from a cattail, I don't remember if I read that story or if someone told it to me, but ever since then, cattail spikes have been special to me, I'd never seen one so I imagined it to be like a penis or a breast, when I came here I found of these clumps of cattails, that's when I realized that the spikes look like poop, I was really happy when I found them, I was really sad when they were uprooted, they had their childhoods uprooted and taken away, they managed to survive a few years without their childhoods, but one day the cattails all came back

to life, I felt like my childhood had returned too, but by that time, I was already an adult, I did something really unfortunate

He said, one day I cut the grass

He said, I got on a big machine and mowed it all down, when I looked over my shoulder, the grass had all completely died under me and the mower, it was so ugly, so cruel that I really regretted it, I regretted it a lot, but over the next week it began to grow again, and by the second week it had grown back to its original height

I said, corpses never die,

I said, at my house, lots of fathers have turned into corpses, they all stay that way, but they're alive, we've watched them, they all stay that way, they groan, they get angry, they have sex with mother, the dogs are the same way, they die, they keep on going, they live, but that's because they're corpses

That's also because we're here at the riverbank

I asked, do you want to have sex with me?

He said, no, I don't, leave me alone, I don't want to have sex, you're clumsy and awkward but you seem like a good girl, you don't have any sexual desire, the only thing you have is the desire to test yourself, from your point of view, I'm just a terribly old man, right? for the moment all I want is to keep rubbing my cock and shoot, we're different from *Conyza sumatrensis* and *Solidago altissima*, so just leave me alone, when I finish shooting, I'll relax and turn to you, then I'll listen carefully and I'll answer all your questions

As he did this, his penis grew bigger and began to glisten, something white flew out of it, the white stuff must have flown three feet into the distance, it smelled raw and sickly sweet, it was the same smell as the spears of seed that were trembling on every side all around the arbor, if this smell was everywhere then we'd have to live in it

Mother, something stinks!

But even if I called out to her, she'd probably just wave a dried-out arm at me

I had to take charge of little brother who was scratching himself all over

I had to get out of there

I had to leave
I was so disappointed in everything that I had gotten pimples
The oil from all those stinky people had seeped into me
But we were not yet corpses
I asked, do you know the name of this kind of grass?,
We looked it up in a plant book once, but it wasn't there
I pointed at the grass with the white spikes of seed
He said, *Paspalum urvillei*
I said, why wasn't it in the plant book?
He said, it was first discovered in 1958 in northern Kyūshū, so it's only newly naturalized here, you know, the word "naturalize" is written with the characters that mean "return" and "change," that is what they call plants that have come from somewhere else and settled down
I said, I've seen that word in the plant book
He said, that's right, that's a word you'd be sure to see in plant books
He looked around with a happy expression and pointed, that's a naturalized plant too
He pointed again, that's another one,
Solidago altissima,
Conyza sumatrensis,
Erigeron canadensis,
The other plants are older,
Some of them came a hundred and fifty years ago when Japan opened up,
Some of them came after World War II,
But this one is different,
Paspalum urvillei is from South America,
It reached here about the time I was born,
We grew up together, the whole time, here on the riverbank,
But neither of us has ever gotten used to the place,
Not *Paspalum urvillei*, not me,
We're not used to the climate or the landscape here, we don't understand the language or what people are saying, neither *Paspalum urvillei* nor me have much to do with people, we don't talk, we don't get accustomed to things, every morning when we wake up, we find we're still in an unfamiliar place
I pointed to the grass with the purple flower, what is this called?

Nearly laughing he said, that's *Verbena brasiliensis*,
It came here around the same time
He danced around as he spoke
It was first found in 1957 in Ōmuda in northwest Kyūshū,
It was growing and spreading and blooming and no one even knew,
Ever since then, we've been living
Together on the riverbank,
Verbena brasiliensis
Paspalum urvillei

That's how I learned two of the names I didn't know
They came fifty years ago to the riverbanks of Japan
Ever since then
They've been trembling in the wind along the riverbank
They've been forming clumps and putting out spikes of seed
Putting out spikes of seed, shaking in the wind, and blooming
Scattering in the wind
Withering and falling over
The whole time on the riverbank
It has lived here
Thinking
I am a stranger
I am a stranger

WE LEAVE THE RIVERBANK AND RETURN TO THE WASTELAND

The summer grass dried up
The air grew completely clear
The parts of the riverbank that had burned started growing fresh, new miscanthus
Miscanthus sacchariflorus started growing everywhere
Growing uniformly, abundantly
I heard the different types of grass on the riverbank whisper, it's all because of the fire, all because of the fire

I got on board
I got on and off then on again
I got on cars, on busses
Then on planes
Then I got off again
While waiting in the airport waiting room, the whole room began to move
And joined up with the airplane
I left mother behind
I left behind the dogs and corpses too
I brought little brother and little sister
In the darkness of the airplane, I heard little brother sob
Then we got off the airplane
The long, long belt clattered forward
I pulled little sister's hand, I urged little brother along the moving sidewalk
Advancing steadily
Advancing steadily, we walked at top speed
As the long, long sidewalk clattered forward

Long ago, we often walked down this sidewalk
It was fun walking on it
Sometimes I'd shake free of mother's hand and race along
The sights had not changed
They were just the same
There were the bodies of immigrants who had run out of energy along the

way and dried up
There were whole families who had nowhere at all to go
And had just laid down there and were sleeping soundly
Mother had once told us, the *immigrants* are dead
Mother had used the unfamiliar word *immigrants*
She said, we're *immigrants* too
There were even more of their corpses than before
There were piles of dried-up corpses in places where there hadn't been any
before
There were reasons for them to come to this country
Even though they might end up like that
Even though they might dry up like that with their children
They had left their lands where they had lived, they had left their languages
Adults who had no choice but to come
Children brought by parents
Who held their hands or carried them along
And when they finally reached the window
They were told,
This isn't where you're supposed to be,
Go home,
Shut your mouth,
Just line up over there
But even so, they came to this country
They left behind their languages
And we were just like them

The man who worked there stared at his computer
How long, he asked,
How long have you been away from this country?
I told him
The man who worked there looked at his computer and gave me a stamp
There is a dirty spot on your passport
The man who worked there told me,
You can't get rid of the dirty spot,
In order to solve this problem,

You have no choice but to transform
So that you look like those who grow here naturally,
Even though you didn't grow here naturally to begin with
(Be carried from your native land to foreign soil, where you will grow wild
and propagate)
Paspalum urvillei
Verbena brasiliensis
Conyza sumatrensis
I picked up little sister
And helped little brother out the door
The rain had just stopped outside
It was as hot and humid as the riverbank we'd left behind
Filled with light
Everything overgrown shone luxuriant green
They spilled out in large numbers
Alexa kawaransis
Erigeron canadensis
Sorghum halepense
Ones who were not born here naturally but that had transformed into ones
who had
Came outside
The passersby and the ones going home
Came outside too
Beside me, *Conyza sumatrensis* started speaking to *Verbena brasiliensis*
Speaking in her awkward language, she said,
How humid it is, shouldn't be like this, not here
Verbena brasiliensis responded even more awkwardly,
It was always rain, all winter was rain
Most rainy year in a hundred years
Verbena brasiliensis began to stutter in her strong accent,
The rrrr.... The rrrr... The rrrrrain
Before finally spitting out the words,
Is just like back home

I had come back here

Thinking we would return to the wasteland
I couldn't come without little brother and little sister
I had watched mother so I knew how to get back home
If I had needed to walk, I don't know if could have done it
But by using trains and busses and planes
We'd get there in no time at all

We left the airport building, and we waited for the bus for a long time while keeping ourselves out of the rain, we got on board the bus and shook back and forth for a long time, the windows of the bus were miserably dirty, the people on board and got off a few at a time, all of the people had left the places where they had been born naturally and had come here, the things growing here were alive, living, life, live oaks, sage thickets and cacti and agave, sage thickets and cacti and agave, when I focused my eyes and looked outside the dirty windows, I could see oak trees standing here and there, burned and dead, they were completely black, there were even some that had fallen over in a big heap

But among the trees I knew to be dead, there were lots and lots of trees that were putting forth thick clusters of new shoots, stretching out their branches and growing quickly, looking closely, I could see their trunks were blackened, I knew the trees had once been burnt black, but now they were covered in green, they had been dyed green, there were growing from the green ground and blooming, it was as if the flowers were seeping out of them, living is more common than dying for plants, even if plants die over and over again, they seem to come back, it doesn't matter how much sage and cacti and agave grow, they still grow sparsely scattered, the sand and rocks show in the rough surface of the earth between them, they grow thick, close to the ground, their leaves are thick, their leaves are white and dry, they are hard to distinguish from the rocks and sand, yet all at once they send up their stems, and at the top of them is a yellow flower
The ground was covered, blooms spread across the earth
The ground was covered, blooms spread across the earth
The ground was covered, blooms spread across the earth
The ground was covered, blooms spread across the earth

Blooms spread across the earth, covering it
Amazing, a truly amazing sight

And that's how we reached the wasteland
Familiar landscapes, trees, and plants
There were things that had grown there naturally
There were things that had come from elsewhere and spread
The man at the riverbank had used the word "naturalize"
A word written with the two characters "return" and "change"
There was a man in front of one of the houses calling out to us
He was one of those people who remembered having come to this land
He was standing there with mud on his hands
He asked, we haven't seen you for ages, where'd you go?
I answered,
We were at the riverbank,
A place with more humidity, more green
The man said,
Everything burned in the mountain fires
It all burned up,
But take a look, things are still alive,
Some things died but some have came back to life,
It's spring,
And this year,
The biggest rain in a hundred years fell,
Things that died, things that didn't,
All of them came back to life all at once,
You too (the man laughed as he said this),
Just now, I was pulling out some ice plants,
They're growing rampant,
That plant originally didn't grow here naturally, someone brought it from
somewhere else, it's really robust, very strong, it's crowding out and killing
all the plants that grow here naturally, our only hope for reclaiming an
environment for the plants that grow here naturally is to get our hands
dirty and tear them out at the roots, we need to eradicate them, but I can't
get them all, I can't eradicate them completely,

I didn't know, didn't know that you could speak,
You speak this language very smoothly,
Almost as if you were born speaking it
(And with that, the man turned the other way)

The ground was covered, blooms spread across the earth
The ground was covered, blooms spread across the earth
The ground was covered, blooms spread across the earth
It was amazing
Living is
More commonplace
Than dying for plants
They come later
They do not end
They do not die
They live from death
They come back to life
They grow again no matter what end they meet
They give birth to any number of children

The familiar house still stood there, it had not fallen into disrepair or grown
forlorn, it was buried in green branches and green leaves, the familiar gate
creaked in a familiar way, and all of us went inside
We heard a voice,
Who is there?
The father whom we had cut off and abandoned was standing there, large
as life, his height and girth seemed much bigger than before, but his face
was ruddy and covered with wrinkles, his hair had grown completely
white, still there was no doubt about it, he was the man who had been
our father, *oh my*, he whispered, extending his arms and taking us into
his embrace, then we understood, there had been mountain fires last year
followed by heavy rain, and as a result, the law of the plants had extended
to this man who had been our father, living had become more commonplace
than dying for him, it had become possible for him to return, the end had
vanished, and it didn't matter how often he died, he could come back to

life again
Father spoke in a voice as grand as a giant tree thousands of years old,
I lost you, I had lost you, but now I'm so happy we've found each other
again, I'll live with you from now on, we'll raise lots of dogs, I want to have
lots, lots more children,
What happened to mama? didn't she come with you?
My little brother said,
She'll be coming later
I said,
That's what she said, but her passport is bad,
She might not be able to come
Our millennia-old father said,
That's right, she must be coming
She'll manage to make it somehow, if she can't, we'll all get flawless
passports and move to the riverbank,
This has been an amazing year,
Look at all this after the rain,
We can have any number of children

The air was moist
The grass spread out
Covered in grass
Moss grew at the base of the trees
Moss grew on the rocks and the sloping earth
Their microscopic stems fertilized in a tumultuous free for all
The large plants stood tall
Undulating and splitting in the wind
Just living and multiplying
Living and multiplying
Multiplying, dying, coming back to life, and multiplying again
In the middle of the wasteland, I spread out my arms and legs wide and
crouched down
And that's how I grew a stem
A bud was born from the tip of the stem
It swelled
And swelled

And opened
And took in everything
The stem continued to grow
Giving birth to one bud after another
They swelled
And opened and withered away
They withered and turned red
Wearing the open flowers and withered flowers upon my body
I continued to grow stems
I grew them with all my might
Trembling in the wind
I looked upward
The sky was not pure blue
It was full of clouds that rushed across the sky
Some of which shone brilliantly in the sun

A GUIDE TO THE PLANTS IN THIS BOOK

Verbena brasiliensis

Common English names: Brazilian verbena, Brazilian vervain
Japanese name: *Arechi-hanagusa* ("wasteland-flowering grass")
Plant family: *Verbenaceae*
Place of origin: South America
Height: 100~200 cm

The stems are heavily textured and, when cut crosswise, reveal a squarish shape. The leaves grow in positions opposite one another and have no coloration patterns, although they do have a deep saw-tooth edge. Toward the top, the stems grow longer and thinner with fewer of the saw-toothed leaves. At that point, the stems divide into many smaller branches and form long, narrow caudal inflorescences with small, pale purple flowers that bloom one after another. The plant flowers from June to August, and is commonly found near harbors, in wasteland, on riverbanks, etc.

Conyza sumatrensis

Common English names: Fleabane, tall fleabane, broad-leaved fleabane
Japanese name: *Ō-arechi-nogiku* ("great-wasteland-wild chrysanthemums")
Plant family: *Asteraceae*
Place of origin: North America
Height: 150~200 cm

The plant is greyish green and covered with fine hairs. It puts out shoots in autumn, winters over with a rosette formation, and resumes growing during the following year. It flowers from July to October, forming a conical spike at the end of the stem and producing many, sparsely scattered compound blooms. This plant, however, does not have any ray florets (the five-petaled flowers that are common to the *Asteraceae* family). The seeds are in the form of a ball of fluff that scatters in the wind. It is commonly found along roadsides, in wasteland, etc.

Solidago altissima

Common English names: Tall goldenrod, late goldenrod
Japanese name: *Seitaka-awadachi-sō* ("tall-foaming-grass")
Plant family: *Asteraceae*

Place of origin: North America
Height: 100~250 cm

This plant is an annual that has naturalized throughout the northern hemisphere. It grows straight up and has no branches, but it does have short hairs on the stalk. The short leaves grow in alternating positions and have a shallow saw-tooth pattern along the edge. The stalks begin growing in spring and flowers from October to November. At the end of the stalk is a large, conical inflorescence with lots of small, dark yellow flowers. The plant commonly grows along river embankments, in vacant lots, in wasteland, etc.

Sorghum halepense

Common English names: Johnson grass, Grama China
Japanese name: *Seiban-morokoshi* ("Tibetan-millet")
Plant family: *Poaceae*
Place of origin: Mediterranean coast
Height: 100~180 cm

This plant grows tall starting in late spring and flourishes by midsummer. It grows so aggressively that even when it is cut back, it recovers quickly and will continue to exert pressure on surrounding plants. The leaves are lanceolate, have white midribs, and look similar to *Miscanthus sinensis* (eulalia grass), but the leaf edges are not rough and will not cut a person's hand. A large seed spike of purplish and yellowish brown forms at the tip of the stem. It flowers from July to September, and is commonly located along roadsides, in wasteland, along riverbanks, etc.

Paspalum urvillei

Common English names: Vasey grass, giant paspalum
Japanese name: *Tachi-suzume-no-hie* ("standing-sparrow-grass")
Plant family: *Poaceae*
Place of origin: South America
Height: 70~150 cm

This plant grows straight up in a cluster of thick stalks. The leaves have slightly rough edges and no hair, but the leaf-sheaths have longish hairs, and the base of the stalks have bristles. Each inflorescence divides into an array of approximately ten to twenty branches, each of which produces two to three small seed spikelets with long, silken tails. The plant flowers from July to September, and is commonly located along roadsides, in wasteland, in vacant lots, etc.

Erigeron canadensis

Common English names: Horseweed, Canadian horseweed, colt's tail, mare's tail, butterweed
Japanese name: *hime-mukashi-yomogi* ("princess-long ago-artemisia")
Plant family: *Asteraceae*
Place of origin: North America
Height: 100~200 cm

This plant arrived in Japan around the time of the opening of Japan in 1868 and spread throughout the country along railroad lines. For this reason, it is sometimes known as "restoration grass" (*goisshingusa*), "Meiji grass" (*meijisō*), "generation-change grass" (*yogawarikusa*), or "railroad grass" (*tetsudōgusa*). It is similar in terms of biology and appearance to *Conyza sumatrensis* (fleabane), but the seed spikes are broader, and there are ray florets on the edges of the flower head. It flowers from July to October, and is common along roadsides, in wasteland, etc.

TRANSLATOR'S NOTES

Page 23, "I don't know what to do": The lines in quotes come directly from Itō's own, long narrative poem "I Am Anjuhimeko" (*Watashi wa Anjuhimeko*), published in 1993. Based on a variant version of the famous medieval legend of Sanshō the Bailiff (Sanshō Dayū) discovered in northeastern Japan, "I Am Anjuhimeko" begins with a description of the tortured relationship between an infant daughter and her mother, who eventually consents to have her daughter killed. This opening portion of the poem, which provides all of the quoted passages, is a piece that Itō often reads at her own poetry readings; in fact, this scene was inspired by an poetry reading she did at Innsbruck. For a translation of "I Am Anjuhimeko," see *Killing Kanoko: Selected Poems of Hiromi Itō*, trans. Jeffrey Angles (Notre Dame, IN: Action Books, 2009), pp. 99-115. For a critical study of Itō's rewriting of this poem, see Jeffrey Angles, "Reclaiming the Unwritten: The Work of Memory in Itō Hiromi's *Watashi wa Anjuhimeko de aru (I Am Anjuhimeko)*," special issue on Itō Hiromi, *U.S.-Japan Women's Journal* 32 (2007): 51-75.

Page 82, "It's Zushio": Zushio is the name of a boy in the medieval legend of Sanshō the Bailiff. In this story, a boy and his older sister Anju are separated from their parents and sold into slavery. Left to their own devices, they grow up on their own, without the help of any authority figures. For a translation of one of the earliest written versions of this medieval legend, see Wondrous Brutal Fictions: *Eight Buddhist Tales from the Early Japanese Puppet Theater*, trans. R. Keller Kimbrough (NY: Columbia University Press, 2013), pp. 23-59.

Page 41, "That thing of yours shut up in a drawer, somewhere in Japan": In Japan, there is a custom of saving the driedup umbilical cord after it falls off a baby.

Page 68, "Michiyuki": *Michiyuki* are lyric compositions that feature prominently in bunraku and kabuki dramas, often serving as one of the climatic scenes in a play. Typically, they describe the scenery that characters encounter while traveling—sometimes while eloping or traveling to a site where they will commit suicide. In Itō's poem, the characters travel in a search for a miraculous, healing hot spring; however, the characters travel and travel in search of a place they cannot find, rendering this *michiyuki* sequence quite anticlimactic and rather funny. Meanwhile, quotes from Neil Young's 1972 song "Harvest," which Itō has worked into the poem, form a sort of background soundtrack. In one passage, as the family approaches the sea on their west, the mother comments that the "Pure Land" is straight ahead. This is a reference to the western paradise that certain sects of Buddhism believe waits for them after death. Such references to the afterlife are common in *michiyuki* sequences, since many of them end with death.

Page 71, "Won't that be Toroku?": These place names are the names of places near Kumamoto, the city in southern Japan where Itō raised her first two daughters and still visits several times each year. The camphor tree mentioned in the text is a local landmark where a sixteenth-century samurai-turned-monk, popularly known as "Jashin-san," was buried.

TRANSLATOR'S ACKNOWLEDGEMENTS

My thanks go to Joyelle McSweeney and Johannes Göransson, the unfailingly energetic editors at Action Books who have been such enthusiastic supporters of Itō's work, both in this translation and in my earlier book of translations *Killing Kanoko: Selected Poems of Hiromi Itō*, which they published in 2009.

Some portions of this translation have appeared in earlier versions in various literary journals. "Mother Leads Us on Board" and "Mother Leads Us to the Wasteland Where We Settle Down" appeared in an early draft on the website *Poetry International Web*. Certain portions of the book have also appeared in the *Asian American Literary Review*. I thank the always wonderful editors Yotsumoto Yasuhiro, Gerald Maa, and Lawrence-Minh Bùi Davis for their support and willingness to allow those portions to be reprinted here.

While working on the final stages of translating this book, I enjoyed the opportunity to share thoughts about it with Ellen Tilton-Cantrell, who wrote extensively about it in her Ph.D. dissertation submitted to Yale in late 2013. Ellen's observations spurred me to refine my own readings of this challenging and playful text, and I thank her for sharing her ideas.

I am especially grateful to Itō's partner, the British-born artist Harold Cohen, who provided the image that appears on the cover of this book. Cohen is internationally known for his experiments with artificial intelligence, particularly his computer program AARON, which he wrote in order to teach computers to create "original" artwork. The cover drawing, called simply "060927," is one of AARON's pieces but drew its inspiration from the many houseplants that fill Itō and Cohen's home in southern California.

Needless to say, the biggest thanks go to Itō Hiromi herself, for all of her support and friendship as I worked on this translation. It is no exaggeration to say that she has enriched my life in more ways than I can name.

HIROMI ITŌ

emerged in the 1980s as the leading voice of Japanese women's poetry with a series of sensational works that depicted women's psychology, sexuality, and motherhood in fresh and dramatic new ways. In the late 1990s, she relocated to southern California, and since then, she has written a number of important, award-winning books about migrancy, relocation, identity, linguistic alienation, aging, and death. Her collection *Kawara arekusa (Wild Grass on the Riverbank)* won the 2006 Takami Jun Prize, which is awarded each year to an outstanding, innovative book of poetry. A selection of her early work appears in *Killing Kanoko: Selected Poems of Hiromi Itō*, translated by Jeffrey Angles (Action Books, 2009).

JEFFREY ANGLES

lives in Kalamazoo, where he is an associate professor of Japanese and translation at Western Michigan University. He is the author of *Writing the Love of Boys* (University of Minnesota Press, 2010) and the award-winning translator of dozens of Japan's most important modern Japanese authors and poets. He believes strongly in the role of translators as social activists, and much of his career has focused on the translation into English of socially engaged, feminist, and queer writers.